Cambridge Elements ⁼

Elements in Perception
edited by
James T. Enns
The University of British Columbia

MELANOPSIN VISION

Sensation and Perception Through Intrinsically Photosensitive Retinal Ganglion Cells

Daniel S. Joyce
University of Nevada, Reno

Kevin W. Houser
Oregon State University

Stuart N. Peirson
University of Oxford

Jamie M. Zeitzer
Stanford University

Andrew J. Zele
Queensland University of Technology

CAMBRIDGE
UNIVERSITY PRESS

CAMBRIDGE
UNIVERSITY PRESS

Shaftesbury Road, Cambridge CB2 8EA, United Kingdom

One Liberty Plaza, 20th Floor, New York, NY 10006, USA

477 Williamstown Road, Port Melbourne, VIC 3207, Australia

314–321, 3rd Floor, Plot 3, Splendor Forum, Jasola District Centre, New Delhi – 110025, India

103 Penang Road, #05–06/07, Visioncrest Commercial, Singapore 238467

Cambridge University Press is part of Cambridge University Press & Assessment, a department of the University of Cambridge.

We share the University's mission to contribute to society through the pursuit of education, learning and research at the highest international levels of excellence.

www.cambridge.org
Information on this title: www.cambridge.org/9781009014878

DOI: 10.1017/9781009029865

First published 2022

A catalogue record for this publication is available from the British Library.

ISBN 978-1-009-01487-8 Paperback
ISSN 2515-0502 (online)
ISSN 2515-0499 (print)

Melanopsin Vision

Sensation and Perception Through Intrinsically Photosensitive Retinal Ganglion Cells

Elements in Perception

DOI: 10.1017/9781009029865
First published online: December 2022

Daniel S. Joyce
University of Nevada, Reno

Kevin W. Houser
Oregon State University

Stuart N. Peirson
University of Oxford

Jamie M. Zeitzer
Stanford University

Andrew J. Zele
Queensland University of Technology

Author for correspondence: Daniel S. Joyce, djoyce@unr.edu

Abstract: Intrinsically photosensitive retinal ganglion cells (ipRGCs) are the most recently discovered photoreceptor class in the human retina. This Element integrates new knowledge and perspectives from visual neuroscience, psychology, sleep science and architecture to discuss how melanopsin-mediated ipRGC functions can be measured and their circuits manipulated. It reveals contemporary and emerging lighting technologies as powerful tools to set mind, brain and behaviour.

Keywords: intrinsically photosensitive retinal ganglion cell, vision, sleep, circadian rhythms, melanopsin

ISBNs: 9781009014878 (PB), 9781009029865 (OC)
ISSNs: 2515-0502 (online), 2515-0499 (print)

Contents

1 Introduction

Life has been evolving on this planet for some 3.5 billion years. For a good portion of that time (depending, for example, on atmospheric conditions), life has been exposed to the regular and alternating pattern of light and dark caused by the Earth's 24-hour rotation on its axis as it orbits the sun. It is perhaps unsurprising then that light is one of the most powerful drivers of behaviour – light influences the way that we think, feel, and act.

The study of these effects of light has a long and rich history that is rooted in medicine. The ancient Greek physician Hippocrates built a solarium and prescribed sunbaths to manage a variety of disorders. The Roman scholar Aulus Cornelius Celsus recommended that sufferers of sickness or melancholy (depression) live in light-filled houses, especially in winter. More recently, Florence Nightingale argued that 'Where there is sun, there is thought', and that hospital wards should be brightly lit, ideally by sunlight. Contemporary medicine now recommends light exposure as a first-line treatment against both seasonal and non-seasonal depressions.

Our understanding of the detection of light is often discussed in relation to an aspect of perception known as 'image-forming' vision mediated via the rods and three cone photoreceptor classes and their classical post-receptoral pathways. Image-forming vision includes the sensory and perceptual aspects of visual experience such as colour, form, or motion, usually discussed in the context of the neurotypical individual. However, lighting also drives diverse aspects of the human experience through setting physiology, arousal, cognition, and mood; responses that are classified as 'non-image-forming'. While these non-image-forming pathways can drive conscious awareness, many of these responses occur over timescales that are much longer than the momentary changes to which our visual perceptual awareness is tuned. This requires a mechanism with a fundamentally distinct temporal tuning to that of the classical visual pathways.

The modern study of non-image-forming vision is grounded in the scientific method and draws strongly from the fields of neuroscience, sleep and circadian sciences, and experimental and applied psychology. Its study has undergone a recent renaissance, where modern psychophysical and neuroscience methods have converged to identify the specialized visual circuits that serve non-image-forming vision and that originate in the retina of the eye. This fifth human photoreceptor class is located in the inner retina and termed the intrinsically photosensitive retinal ganglion cells (ipRGCs). Phototransduction initiated by the intrinsic melanopsin photopigment expressed by ipRGCs was initially shown to have a unique, characteristic temporal response: a slow onset followed by a sustained depolarization that is maintained even after the stimulating light is switched off. In addition to their unique intrinsic photoresponse, ipRGCs extrinsically mediate signals originating in outer retinal rod and cone photoreceptors. The ipRGCs therefore possess temporal characteristics suited to sensing both transient changes in light but also day-length changes.

These non-image-forming pathways project to over a dozen diverse efferent brain targets, and in this Element we evaluate the current state of knowledge for these functional melanopsin pathways that set pupil size, perceptual vision, circadian rhythms and sleep/wake transitions, and arousal, mood, and cognition. We focus on delineating findings in primates (including humans) from those of other model organisms. Indeed, these non-image-forming signals appear fundamentally entwined with the human condition and we discuss lightscapes that not only serve image-forming vision, but that target non-image-forming physiology to positively modify health and behaviour. Physiologically targeted electric light sources have future applications as 'photoceuticals', with therapeutic effects analogous to those of pharmaceuticals and designed with similar considerations concerning disease specificity, dosage, and timing. Given the new developments in the understanding of ipRGCs and their image-forming and non-image-forming projections, we provide a contemporary account of the importance of light and melanopsin function for brain, mind, and behaviour.

2 Evidence for the Non-image-Forming Pathways and Novel Retinal Photoreceptors

The non-image-forming pathways are a relatively new discovery, and were initially a contentious one at that, because the visual pathways have long been studied. For some 150 years, vision scientists had modelled human visual perception by the rod and cone photoreceptor classes (Maxwell 1855, König and Dieterici 1893, von Helmholtz 1896, Schrödinger 1925). As early as the start of the twentieth century, however, evidence was mounting for a non-image-forming visual pathway that was at least partially independent from rod and cone photoreception. In the 1920s, a graduate student named Clyde Keeler was working with mice that were severely degenerate in their outer retina, lacking rod and cone photoreceptors, making these mice functionally blind (Keeler et al. 1928). Despite this, the mice still demonstrated robust and repeatable pupillary light constrictions (Keeler 1927). Potentially, another class of photoreceptors could be present in the retina, one that was necessarily able to survive outer retinal degeneration and that projected to the pupil control pathway. On the other hand, it was possible that the outer retinal degeneration was simply incomplete, leaving a small but functionally significant population of rod or cone photoreceptors that could still drive pupillary responses to light. This was the most parsimonious explanation at the time, and it was not until many decades later that concerted and compelling evidence was presented for the non-image-forming pathways.

In mammals, light detected by the eye is the primary time cue that synchronizes the circadian rhythms of activity and rest – a process termed photoentrainment. The twilight transitions of light that occur at dawn and dusk play a key role, adjusting the phase of the master circadian clock in the hypothalamic suprachiasmatic nuclei (SCN) (Roenneberg and Foster 1997, Hughes et al. 2015, Walmsley et al. 2015). Evening light exposure results in a phase delay in the circadian clock, whereas light exposure in the morning produces phase advances. In this way, light adjusts the phase of the internal circadian clock to the external light/dark (LD) environment.

Research during the 1990s on the non-image-forming effects of light provided important clues that the mammalian eye may contain an additional photoreceptor. The evidence came from studies on retinally degenerate mice, in which rods and most of the cones were lost. Even though these animals were visually blind, their circadian phase-shifting responses to light persisted (Provencio and Foster 1995, Yoshimura and Ebihara 1996), commensurate with Keeler's observations many years earlier permissive of an additional photoreceptive mechanism. When exposed to a brief light pulse (~15 mins) in the early night, mice delay their activity onset the following day. This response is intensity dependent, enabling an irradiance-response curve (IRC) to be constructed (Figure 1), in a similar manner to a drug dose-response curve. Such curves have a characteristic sigmoid shape, which moves to the left when sensitivity increases and to the right when sensitivity declines, so that a different dose of light is required to evoke an equivalent biological response (see the caption of Figure 1) (Peirson et al. 2005). When studied in this manner, the blind mice showed circadian responses, but with a spectral sensitivity shifted to shorter wavelengths and a reduced sensitivity to irradiance (Yoshimura and Ebihara 1996). The photoreceptors mediating circadian entrainment were certainly ocular, as loss of the eye abolished all responses to light (Nelson and Zucker 1981, Foster et al. 1991). However, as with Keeler, a potential explanation for these findings was that these circadian responses could be driven by the few remaining cones that survived.

Subsequent studies in retinally degenerate mice in which cones were also genetically lesioned demonstrated that both circadian phase shifting and melatonin suppression were retained in the absence of rods and cones (Freedman et al. 1999). Moreover, an action spectrum on the pupillary light response in these mice demonstrated that this was driven by a photopigment with a peak

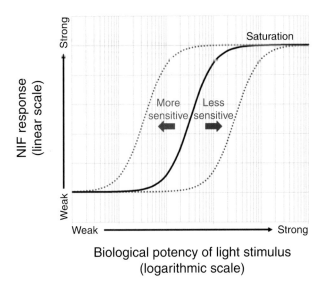

Figure 1 Example IRC. A log-linear relationship typically exists between light stimuli and non-image-forming responses, such as the suppression by light of the circadian hormone melatonin in humans (Zeitzer et al. 2000) (solid curve). In practice, a complex interplay between stimulus parameters, intra-individual and inter-individual factors result in non-image-forming IRCs that are not static: the physical parameters of the light (intensity, duration, spectral power distribution (SPD)), the individual's light exposure history, and the timing of the light exposure relative to circadian phase can all impact the IRC. When the sensitivity of the system increases, the sigmoid curve shifts to the left wherein the same light stimulus becomes more effective (or more biologically potent) in eliciting a non-image-forming response. When the sensitivity of the system decreases, the sigmoid shifts to the right and the biological potency of the stimulus is reduced. Response threshold (below which no response occurs), saturation (above which the response does not increase in magnitude), and slope of the relationship (determining the magnitude of response change to a unit change in stimulus) may also vary (not shown).

sensitivity (λ_{max}) of 479 nm, which corresponded to none of the known mouse visual pigments (Lucas et al. 2001). Together, these studies provided the key evidence for a novel retinal photoreceptor in mammals.

3 Intrinsically Photosensitive Retinal Ganglion Cells

There are some 30 types of ganglion cells identified in mammals (Sanes and Masland 2015). They relay signals that originate in the photoreceptors in the retina to higher brain centres via their axons that form the optic nerve that attaches the eye to the brain. Ganglion cells were not known to be photosensitive and so it was remarkable that the novel photoreceptor system identified in mice consisted of a subset of ganglion cells that uniquely express the photopigment melanopsin (OPN4), now known as intrinsically photosensitive retinal ganglion cells (Figures 2 and 3) (Provencio et al. 2000, 2002, Hattar et al. 2002). Melanopsin is named because it was initially isolated from melanophores in amphibian skin, and is an opsin-vitamin A type photopigment that shares many characteristics with invertebrate visual pigments (Provencio et al. 1998b). In the mammalian retina, ipRGCs form a syncytium or photoreceptive net across the retina (Provencio et al. 2000, 2002). These ipRGCs project directly to the rodent SCN and other brain regions associated with non-image-forming responses and have a peak response to light at ~480 nm that appears blueish-cyanish (Berson et al. 2002, Hattar et al. 2003). In the literature, these cells have also been referred to as photosensitive retinal ganglion cells (pRGCs) or melanopsin retinal ganglion cells (mRGCs).

Following the identification of ipRGCs, it was initially thought that the image-forming effects of light were independently mediated by rods/cones while the

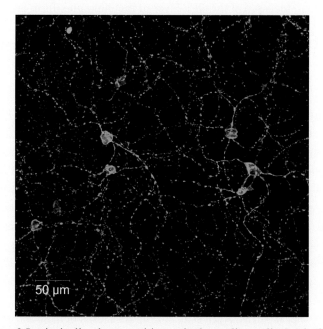

Figure 2 Intrinsically photosensitive retinal ganglion cells. Intrinsically photosensitive retinal ganglion cells form a syncytium or photoreceptive net within the mammalian retina. Flatmount image of mouse retina immunostained for melanopsin. Image courtesy of Steven Hughes.

Figure 3 Stitched micrograph labelling melanopsin-expressing cells of the mouse retina, focussed at the OFF layer of the inner plexiform layer (IPL). Mice were a cross between the Opn4-driven tamoxifen-inducible Cre mouse line (Opn4 [CreERT2]) and the Z/AP reporter line, allowing controlled expression of AP on the plasma membrane of melanopsin-expressing cells (Joo et al. 2013). Image courtesy of Shih-Kuo Alen Chen.

non-image-forming effects of light were mediated by melanopsin. However, studies of transgenic mice that lacked melanopsin found that the mice could still entrain their circadian rhythms, had only mild deficits in circadian phase shifting, and still retained pupillary responses to bright light (Panda et al. 2002, Ruby et al. 2002, Lucas et al. 2003). Therefore, extrinsic rod and cone inputs to ipRGCs were able to drive these responses even in the absence of melanopsin. When the melanopsin ipRGCs are lesioned, non-visual responses no longer occur, demonstrating that ipRGCs provide the primary conduit for this pathway in mice (Guler et al. 2008) and in non-human primates (Ostrin et al. 2018). Moreover, ipRGCs have been shown to mediate visual responses independent of the rod and cone pathways in mice (Ecker et al. 2010, Schmidt et al. 2014) and in humans (Zele et al. 2018c, Allen et al. 2019b). As a result of these and a range of electrophysiological studies on the responses of melanopsin ipRGCs both with and without rod or cone input (Dacey et al. 2005), it is now clear that the response of ipRGCs depends upon both their intrinsic melanopsin-driven photoresponses and extrinsic rod/cone input (Figure 4) (Markwell et al. 2010, Lucas et al. 2014).

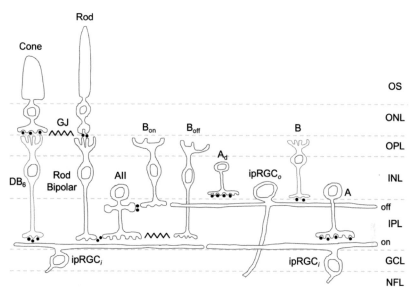

Figure 4 Intrinsically photosensitive retinal ganglion cell retinal circuits. Inner stratifying photosensitive ganglion cell bodies (ipRGC$_i$s) are located in the ganglion cell layer (GCL) with their dendrites stratifying along the extreme inner strata of the inner plexiform layer (IPL). Outer stratifying photosensitive ganglion cell bodies (ipRGC$_o$s) are co-located in the GCL and the inner nuclear layer (INL) with their dendrites in the extreme outer strata of the IPL. Cone signals are transmitted to ipRGCs via DB$_6$ cone bipolar cells. Synaptic contact also occurs between ipRGCs and dopaminergic amacrine (A$_d$), bipolar (B), and amacrine cells (A), including within an S-cone circuit in primate retina. Rod input to ipRGCs may be transmitted via rod–cone gap junctions (GJs) and the DB$_6$ bipolar cells; extrinsic rod inputs via the ON rod bipolar, AII amacrine cells, and ON (B$_{on}$) and OFF (B$_{off}$) cone bipolars is yet to be determined in primates, although synaptic contact has been shown between rod bipolars and ipRGC$_i$ in rats. Abbreviations: nerve fibre layer (NFL); outer nuclear layer (ONL); outer plexiform layer (OPL); outer segment (OS). Figure from Markwell et al. (2010), copyright © 2022 Optometry Australia, reprinted by permission of Taylor & Francis Ltd, www.tandfonline.com on behalf of 2022 Optometry Australia.

3.1 Intrinsically Photosensitive Retinal Ganglion Cell Diversity and Projections in Rodents

Rather than just a single class of circadian photoreceptor, the ipRGC system has remarkable complexity. Electrophysiological responses of mouse ipRGCs to light reveal transient, sustained, and repeatable responses to the same stimulus

(Sekaran et al. 2003, Tu et al. 2005). Mouse ipRGCs show a range of anatomical diversity, leading to an initial classification of three subtypes (M1, M2, and M3). Improved transgenic reporter models revealed additional subtypes, so that today, M1–M5 subtypes of mouse ipRGC are recognized (Ecker et al. 2010, Hu et al. 2013), with an M6 subtype recently identified (Quattrochi et al. 2019). These subtypes have different levels of melanopsin expression, varying degrees of intrinsic photosensitivity, distinct anatomical morphology, and even different brain projections that appear to underlie the range of different non-image-forming light responses (Schmidt et al. 2011, Sand et al. 2012, Hughes et al. 2016). For example, there are differences between the ipRGC subtype projections to the SCN (mediating circadian responses) and the olivary pretectal nuclei (OPN; mediating pupillary responses). Tracer studies have shown that M1 cells account for around 80% of SCN-projecting ipRGCs, with the remaining 20% presumed to be M2. By contrast, M1 cells account for 45% of ipRGCs projecting to the OPN, with M2 cells accounting for 55% (Baver et al. 2008). And even within these ipRGC subtypes, differences appear to exist. For example, M1 cells can be further subdivided into those expressing the Brn3b transcription factor and those that do not, and these cells underlie different contributions to circadian and pupillary responses to light (Chen et al. 2011). Furthermore, a recent detailed study of the cellular diversity of M1 ipRGCs in mice has shown that these cells individually show quite different and narrow ranges of light sensitivity, but together provide a population representation of light over a wide dynamic range from moonlight to bright sunlight (Milner and Do 2017). It is unclear whether a similar mechanism occurs in humans.

The melanopsin gene (*Opn4*) has also been shown to exhibit diversity, with two independent genes found in most non-mammalian vertebrates (termed *Opn4x* and *Opn4m*) (Bellingham et al. 2006). An even more extreme example is found in teleost fishes, where five separate melanopsin genes have been identified, resulting in a form of melanopsin being expressed in every major cell type of the teleost retina (Davies et al. 2011, 2015). Even in mammals where a single melanopsin gene is present, alternative splicing results in long and short isoforms with differential expression patterns within melanopsin subtypes (Pires et al. 2009). These expression patterns result in different contributions to behavioural responses to light (Jagannath et al. 2015).

The use of retrograde labelling and transgenic reporter mouse lines showed that the melanopsin ipRGCs project to the SCN, but also other areas associated with non-image-forming responses to light, including the OPN, intergeniculate leaflet (IGL), and the ventral lateral geniculate (vLGN). Detailed anatomical mapping of ipRGC pathways identified a remarkable diversity of projections (Figure 5), suggesting a much wider role in non-image-forming responses than

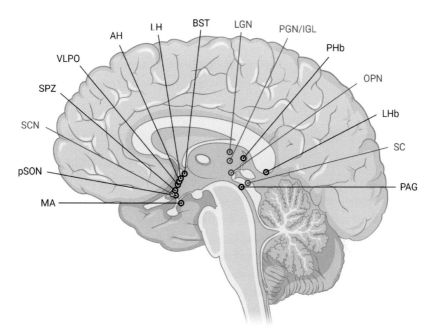

Figure 5 Central projections of ipRGCs. To date, most projections have been identified in rodents (black), with relatively few projections confirmed in primates (red), and fewer still confirmed in humans (blue). Abbreviations: anterior hypothalamic nucleus (AH); bed nucleus of the stria terminalis (BST); lateral geniculate nucleus (LGN); lateral hypothalamus (LH); peri-supraoptic nucleus (pSON); periaqueductal grey (PAG); perihabenular nucleus (PHb); pregeniculate nucleus (primates)/IGL (rodents) (PGN/IGL); ventrolateral preoptic area (VLPO). Figure created with BioRender.com.

initially envisaged (Hattar et al. 2006). This includes the lateral nucleus, peri-supraoptic nucleus, subparaventricular zone (SPZ) of the hypothalamus, the medial amygdala (MA), the lateral habenula (LHb; now known to be the perihabenula region) (Fernandez et al. 2018), posterior limitans nucleus, the superior colliculus (SC), the periaqueductal grey, and even weak projections to the dorsal lateral geniculate nucleus (dLGN) (Hattar et al. 2006). With the identification of mouse M4 and M5 ipRGCs, more extensive projections to the SC and dLGN were also identified (Ecker et al. 2010). Recent studies have shown that M5 ipRGCs project to the dLGN and may provide colour opponent signals (ultraviolet excitatory, green inhibitory) to visual pathways (Stabio et al. 2018), illustrating the overlap between classical visual pathways and the melanopsin ipRGC system. Studying these contributions of ipRGCs to visual function is complicated by differences in visual function between rodents and primates, and requires different methodological approaches when studying melanopsin-mediated function in humans. For example, mouse visual acuity is poor and mice would be classified as legally (but not completely) blind when evaluated against human visual performance standards (Grünert and Martin 2021).

3.2 Intrinsically Photosensitive Retinal Ganglion Cell in Primates

Alongside its discovery in frog and rodents, melanopsin was identified in the macaque and human inner retina (Provencio et al. 2000). These ipRGCs that express melanopsin correspond to the sparse giant class of ganglion cells and, in humans, three ipRGC subtypes have been identified that are homologues to the mouse M1, M2, and M3 and M4 subtypes (Liao et al. 2016, Esquiva et al. 2017, Hannibal et al. 2017, Nasir-Ahmad et al. 2017, Ortuño-Lizarán et al. 2018, Mure et al. 2019). Anatomical studies of the marmoset retina show a similar pattern of melanopsin expression (Jusuf et al. 2007, Masri et al. 2019). Detailed anatomical characterization of human ipRGCs indicates that at least some degree of cellular diversity also occurs in the human retina (Dacey et al. 2005, Liao et al. 2016, Hannibal et al. 2017), supported by a diversity of cellular responses (Mure et al. 2019). Old World monkeys, such as macaques, have trichromatic vision that is similar to that of humans (Jacobs et al. 1996); the macaque melanopsin photopigment has λ_{max} at ~482 nm when measured in vitro (Dacey et al. 2005) and through contributions to pupillary responses (Gamlin et al. 2007). The central projections of macaque ipRGCs include the SCN, the lateral geniculate, the olivary pretectal nucleus, the nucleus of the optic tract, and the SC (Hannibal et al. 2014). The projections to the lateral geniculate are of particular interest and suggest that signals from ipRGCs may converge with the classical visual pathways that underpin image-forming vision (Dacey et al. 2005).

The gene that is encoding human melanopsin has also been shown to exhibit a range of polymorphisms, leading to functionally relevant changes in protein structure. A missense mutation (P10L) of human melanopsin is associated with seasonal affective disorder (Roecklein et al. 2009). Subsequent studies have suggested that other human melanopsin variants may contribute to differences in sleep onset and chronotype (Roecklein et al. 2012), and may also contribute to differences in pupillary responses to light (Lee et al. 2013, 2014, Roecklein et al. 2013). In addition to these associations, in vitro studies have shown that several human melanopsin variants have significantly altered signal transduction (Rodgers et al. 2018b) and in vivo expression of these human variants in mouse ipRGCs can lead to altered ipRGC responses to light (Rodgers et al. 2018a).

3.3 Spectral Sensitivity of Melanopsin-Expressing ipRGCs

The human eye has five spectrally distinct photoreceptor classes with broad, overlapped spectral responses (Figure 6a). It is their relative activation levels that ultimately determine human image forming and non-image-forming sensitivity to light across a large range of lighting conditions spanning some 12 log units of illumination. Rods have the highest sensitivity to dim lighting and are the most abundant human photoreceptor class (~91 million rods), the L-, M-, and S-cones signal at moderate to bright lighting conditions and underpin colour perception (~4.5 million cones), while the ipRGCs are the scarcest photoreceptor class (~3,000 ipRGCs). The peak spectral response of the human melanopsin pathway is ~480 nm as estimated via heterologous gene expression of the photopigment (Bailes and Lucas 2013), measures of non-image-forming circadian function (al Enezi et al. 2011), and pupil responses of both sighted and blind individuals (Gamlin et al. 2007, Gooley et al. 2012, Adhikari et al. 2015b). This sensitivity positions melanopsin between the short wavelength sensitive cone opsin (expressed in S-cones) and rhodopsin (expressed in rods) and relatively far from the λ_{max} of human vision (under photopic conditions) that occurs at longer wavelengths in the greenish-appearing region of the visible spectrum at ~555 nm. This is known as the luminous efficiency function, $V(\lambda)$, corresponding to the weighted sum of medium- and long-wavelength-sensitive cone inputs to the magnocellular pathway in the LGN under photopic conditions (Lennie et al. 1993, Lucas et al. 2014). The luminous efficiency function was determined using psychophysical procedures such as heterochromatic flicker photometry (HFP), and satisfies Abney's law of additivity where the luminance of a light of a mixture of wavelengths is the sum of the luminances of its monochromatic constituents. The luminous efficiency function is the basis of many lighting measures including luminous intensity (candela), luminous flux (lumens), and illuminance (lux). Because $V(\lambda)$ is based on a physiologic circuit that is largely distinct from that of ipRGCs, it does not reflect the response of melanopsin ipRGCs or their contributions to image-forming or non-image-forming function. As such, a melanopsin-weighted lux measurement was proposed to account for non-image-forming responses to light (al Enezi et al. 2011, Lucas et al. 2014), with the CIE (Commission Internationale de l'Éclairage; an international standards body concerned with quantifying the physical and psychophysical attributes of light including the measurement, sensation, and perception of colour) formally adopting a system of photometry for ipRGC-influenced responses to light (Commission Internationale de l'Éclairage 2018). The difference between the spectral sensitivity of the image-forming and non-image-forming systems has attracted a great deal of attention from the lighting

(a)

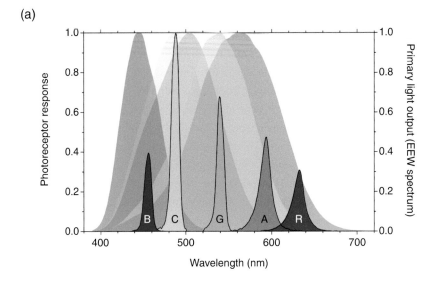

(b)

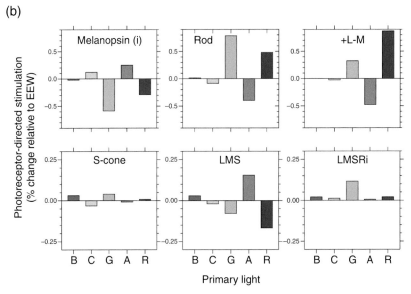

Figure 6 Spectral response of the human eye, exemplar primary light output spectrums, and their application in photoreceptor-directed stimulation during silent substitution. (a) Shaded areas show the normalized spectral sensitivities of the five human photoreceptors as per CIE S 026:2018. Overlayed are the spectral outputs of five independently controllable narrowband primary lights that therefore have strongly saturated hues (B, Blue; C, Cyan; G, Green; A, Amber; R, Red), as per Cao et al. (2015), scaled to produce a light metameric to an equal energy white (EEW) spectrum for the CIE 1964 10 degree standard

industry, in order to develop integrative lighting solutions that address both image-forming and non-image-forming responses and produce positive physio-logical, psychological, and behavioural outcomes for humans (Commission Internationale de l'Éclairage 2019, Houser et al. 2020, Houser and Esposito 2021).

Due to the cellular diversity of the ipRGC system and the range of biological responses it is known to mediate, it is still to be determined if a single spectral sensitivity function is suitable to describe all melanopsin-mediated responses to light. For example, studies in mice have shown that due to the extrinsic rod/cone input to melanopsin ipRGCs, circadian responses to light only correspond to melanopsin λ_{max} (~480 nm) in the absence of rods and cones (Hattar et al. 2003). In contrast, responses are more sensitive to light around 500 nm in the intact murine retina where rod/cone inputs are retained (Provencio & Foster 1995, Yoshimura and Ebihara 1996, van Oosterhout et al. 2012). These data indicate a role for rods, which have also been shown to play an important role in circadian entrainment (Altimus et al. 2010, Lall et al. 2010). The light intensity used, adaptation level based upon prior light history, and the temporal characteristics of the stimulus can all influence the relative contributions of melanopsin, rods, and cones to both non-image-forming (Lucas et al. 2014) and image-forming responses to light (Zele et al. 2019b).

A photoreceptor's spectral response determines its probability of quantal catch as a function of wavelength (Figure 6). Following the principle of

---

Caption for Figure 6 (cont.)

observer. Lights are said to be metameric when they have different SPDs but entail the same photoreceptor quantal catch (and so photoreceptor responses to each light) across all of the photoreceptor classes. This EEW spectrum is an example of a reference background adapting chromaticity. The photoreceptor-directed silent substitutions are referenced to this background as either increments or decrements. The photoreceptor excitations relative to photopic luminance with a 2:1 L:M cone ratio are specified as $l = L/(L+M) = 0.6667$, $m = M/(L+M) = 0.3333$, $s = S/(L+M) = 1$, $r = R/(L+M) = 1$, and $i = I/(L+M) = 1$ for 1 photopic Troland light metameric to the EEW spectrum. (b) Required percentage output changes of the five primary lights relative to the background EEW spectrum to generate a 15% Weber contrast increment in six different photoreceptor-directed stimuli during the test phase, without changing the excitations of the unmodulated photoreceptors (e.g., the top left panel demonstrates a melanopsin (i) modulation that is silent for (does not change) the excitations of the rhodopsin, L-, M- and S-cone opsins relative to the background EEW spectrum).

univariance (Rushton 1972), a photoreceptor cannot necessarily differentiate between a change in stimulus wavelength and a change in stimulus intensity because various combinations of stimulus wavelength and intensity can result in the same quantal catch. As a result, decreasing the blue light emission of a light source will reduce the level of melanopsin activation, but even blue-depleted light sources will still be capable of driving melanopsin ipRGC responses if of sufficiently high irradiance. A blunt approach such as reducing the correlated colour temperature (CCT) of a light source may lessen melatonin suppression by driving the maximum emission of the light to longer wavelengths, though intentional spectral engineering enables CCT to be decoupled from melanopsin activation (Feigl et al. 2022). More sophisticated psychophysical methods to decouple photoreceptor inter-relations are discussed in Section 4.

4 Methodological Considerations for the Experimental Control of Photoreception in Humans

Combining lighting and computer technology with our increasing knowledge of the ipRGC pathways mean that it is possible to selectively modulate ipRGC photoreceptors using specialized light-adapted psychophysical methods. Stimulus generators can separate the melanopsin inputs to human vision from those of the rhodopsin and cone-opsin contributions to perception, pupillary processes, or other non-image-forming functions using a method known as silent substitution (Estevez and Spekreijse 1982, Shapiro et al. 1996). With silent substitution, the number of primary lights must be no fewer than the number of active photoreceptors (Zele and Cao 2015) and so sophisticated optical apparatus have been developed using five, independently controlled narrowband primary lights (e.g., using LED and interference filter combinations) of different peak wavelengths (Cao et al. 2015). In this method, the radiance of each primary light is suitably adjusted to generate a reference background adapting chromaticity (e.g., one often metameric to an equal energy white spectrum, EEW; Figure 6a), and a test state that actively changes the excitation of one (or more) photoreceptors while keeping the other excitations constant (Figure 6b). The adapting background chromaticity with its specified LMSRi photoreceptor excitation (L = L-cone opsin; M = M-cone opsin; S = S-cone opsin; R = Rhodopsin; i = Melanopsin) then transitions over time to the test state that alters the quantal catch of one photoreceptor class (e.g., delta melanopsin; Δi) while retaining a metameric match to the reference background across the other four photoreceptor classes (e.g., S, M, L, and R). Because the quantal catch of the other photoreceptor classes does not change between the reference and test fields, this is a 'silent substitution' for those classes that do not detect any change between stimuli. The primary light outputs can be adjusted to make the silent substitution visible to one or more photoreceptor combinations to facilitate the study of photoreceptor interactions, with applications in psychophysics, pupillometry, electrophysiology, and functional imaging.

The 5-primary silent-substitution method has an advantage in that the trichromatic visual system is measured intact in vivo in order to provide an ecologically valid model for probing melanopsin function that can be independent of the effects of the rod and cone pathways, or in concert with them (Cao et al. 2015). Importantly, silent-substitution studies do not require assumptions about the impacts of ophthalmic or neurological disease on retinal (and cortical) networks, the effects of pharmacological intervention, or transgenic or chemogenic manipulation of melanopsin function and its dependence and interaction with rod and cone function. For research purposes, pupil dilation of the test eye (mydriasis) using pharmacological agents, or the use of an optical instrument set in Maxwellian view to converge the stimuli down to the plane of a small artificial pupil (Westheimer 1966), is preferred. One reason is because non-converging Newtonian view systems using undilated pupils allow the retinal illumination to vary with pupil diameter due to changes in accommodation and convergence and due to lighting conditions with different melanopsin excitations. Such effects can be problematic because they inadvertently introduce subtle, illumination-dependent changes in visual contrast sensitivity that confound the outcome measures. Some 4- and 5-primary systems merge the outputs of two 3-primary displays but co-opt one primary (e.g., red or green) for two states using optical filters (Yang et al. 2018, Allen et al. 2019a, Hexley et al. 2020), but this can result in limited rhodopsin and melanopsin gamuts. Although four primary stimulus generators are effective for providing full photoreceptor control to study mesopic rod–cone interactions in trichromats (Pokorny et al. 2004), or of all four photoreceptor classes in dichromats (people with melanopsin, rods, and two of the three cone opsins), the 4-primary system cannot control melanopsin–rod interactions in the trichromat, nor rod–cone interactions that are known to alter visual sensitivity (Zele and Cao 2015).

Practically, implementing silent substitution is not a trivial task, and a key issue when separating the melanopsin photoresponse from the more sensitive cone pathways is to ensure that stimulus artefacts (intrusion) arising from errors in the silent substitution are minimized. This requires extremely careful physical light and individual observer calibrations (Uprety et al. 2021). The observer corrections can minimize the individual differences in the inert optical pigments (e.g., lens, macular pigment) and photoreceptor spectral sensitivities between the individual and the CIE standard observer sensitivity functions (Baraas and Zele 2016, Mollon et al. 2017, Spitschan et al. 2017). In practice, these individual differences can be effectively determined using HFP (Lennie et al. 1993, Uprety et al. 2021).

One such intrusion is caused by penumbral cones in the shadow of retinal blood vessels (Horiguchi et al. 2013). Silent substitution is designed for open-field photoreceptors that are unobstructed, whereas the retinal vasculature differentially absorbs light and casts shadows across nearby photoreceptors, known as the Purkinje tree (Purkyně 1823). The resultant difference in quantal catch between open-field, umbral and penumbral cones can change the precision of silent substitution in those retinal locations. The penumbral cones may be more sensitive to melanopsin-directed stimuli at higher temporal frequencies and photopic illuminations (without macular blocking) than is the intrinsic melanopsin photoresponse (Horiguchi et al. 2013, Cao et al. 2015, Spitschan et al. 2015). This intrusion can be minimized by restricting stimuli to lower temporal frequencies (Spitschan et al. 2015), using steady-light adaptation (Yamakawa et al. 2019) or through the application of temporal white noise to desensitise unwanted photoreceptor intrusions (Hathibelagal et al. 2016, Zele et al. 2018c).

The intrusion levels of the uncontrolled photoreceptor contrasts should be reported, and their effects evaluated experimentally in control conditions, to establish their contribution to the hypothesized visual or non-visual melanopsin effects (Adhikari et al. 2019b, Zele et al. 2019b). To the advantage of the experimenter, the photoreceptor isolation can be evaluated using the pupil light response (PLR) because different stimulus combinations produce characteristic amplitudes and timings, consistent with their initiation by different photoreceptor classes (Tsujimura and Tokuda 2011, Spitschan et al. 2014, Cao et al. 2015, Barrionuevo and Cao 2016, Zele et al. 2018c, 2019a). An L-cone, M-cone, or melanopsin-directed flicker pupil response is excitatory and antagonistic to the inhibitory, S-cone-directed flicker pupil response (Figure 7a) (Spitschan et al. 2014, Cao et al. 2015, Zele et al. 2018c) in accordance with the (L+M)-ON and S-OFF response property of primate ipRGCs (Dacey et al. 2005). A melanopsin-directed incremental pulse will drive a slow and sustained constriction with a long latency (~290 ms longer than the cone-directed PLR) and characteristic post-illumination pupil response (PIPR) that persists following stimulus offset (Figure 7b) (Zele et al. 2019a). This melanopsin signal sets the steady-state pupil diameter during prolonged light exposure (Tsujimura et al. 2010). In comparison, cone-directed pulses cause transient pupil constrictions that rapidly redilate to baseline (Figure 7b, L+M cones) (Barbur et al. 1992, Gamlin et al. 1998, Tsujimura et al. 2001, Young and Kimura 2008, Zele et al. 2019a). These extrinsic rod and cone inputs to ipRGCs and their interactions with the intrinsic melanopsin photoresponse involve both linear and

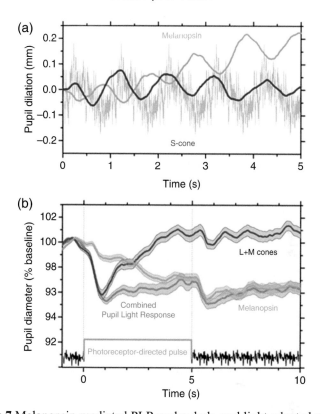

Figure 7 Melanopsin-mediated PLR under dark- and light-adapted viewing conditions. (a) Light-adapted (2000 photopic Troland) melanopsin-directed pupil flicker response (green line) to a 1 Hz stimulus with penumbral cone silencing temporal white noise (grey line) are counterphrase (opponent in action) to the S-cone-directed pupil response (blue line) that paradoxically dilates the pupil with increasing irradiance. Modified after Zele et al. (2018c). (b) Melanopsin-directed pupil responses, +L+M cone luminance-directed responses, and the combined +L+M cone and melanopsin-directed response measured during light adaptation. Each pupil trace shows the average ±95% confidence limits of four observers (100 trials per observer). Temporal white noise is presented during the pre- and post-stimulus periods (bottom line) to limit the penumbral cone intrusion. Modified after Zele et al. (2019a).

non-linear processes (Howarth et al. 1991, Barrionuevo et al. 2014, 2018, Barrionuevo and Cao 2016, Zele et al. 2019a) and the antagonism between opponent cone signals together determines the PLR amplitude and timing (Barbur et al. 1992, Murray et al. 2018, Woelders et al. 2018). The inner and outer retinal signals combine to generate the light-adapted pupil response (Figure 7b, combined pupil response). That pupil responses are attenuated in people without functional geniculostriate projections to the primary visual cortex also points to an additional cortical site for processing chromatic signals (Barbur et al. 1992, 1998).

5 The Pupil as a Measure of Non-image-Forming Vision

The eye's pupil is an aperture bordered by the iris that can provide about 1 log unit of attenuation of the retinal illuminance (Lowenstein and Loewenfeld 1969). Pupil size is set dynamically by two sets of smooth muscle that act in opposition to one another; the circular sphincter pupillae muscle contracts to constrict the pupil and is under control of the parasympathetic nervous system, whereas the radial dilator pupillae muscle contracts to widen the pupil and is controlled by the sympathetic nervous system (Lowenstein and Loewenfeld 1969, Gamlin 2003). While pupil responses have been studied for centuries, advances in computing have enabled real-time quantitative analyses of pupil size at high spatial and temporal resolution, and are now deployed clinically (Kawasaki and Kardon 2007, Feigl and Zele 2014, Kelbsch et al. 2019). Pupillometry has many advantages as a measure of the ipRGC pathway because it can be inexpensive, rapid, does not require individual observer calibration, and is immune to malingering as it measures a reflex arc not under volitional control – although there are rare counterexamples (Eberhardt et al. 2021), including as an adaptation to extreme environments (Gislén et al. 2003). Pupillometry is especially versatile, it can probe bottom-up (afferent pathways) and top-down (e.g., cognitive) control of the pupil as well as index autonomic state (Lowenstein and Loewenfeld 1969). A rapidly increasing body of work isolates and quantifies non-image-forming melanopsin control of the human pupil.

Intrinsically photosensitive retinal ganglion cells form the afferent pupil control pathway in non-human primates (Gamlin et al. 2007, Ostrin et al. 2018) via subcortical projections through the pretectum, specifically the olivary pretectal nucleus (Hannibal et al. 2014) to the Edinger–Westphal nucleus (Pierson and Carpenter 1974, Gamlin and Reiner 1991). In humans, the most readily accessible biomarker of melanopsin function is the sustained constriction following light offset known as the post-illumination pupil response (Figure 8) (Adhikari et al. 2015b). It is typically measured in the dark because light adaptation drives the pupil to a relatively miotic state that reduces its available dynamic range of movement (Joyce et al. 2016a, Kelbsch et al. 2019). The melanopsin-mediated PIPR can be reliably separated from rod and cone inputs using a stimulus sequence including a combination of narrowband stimulus lights, which have a narrow SPD and appears as a strongly saturated hue.

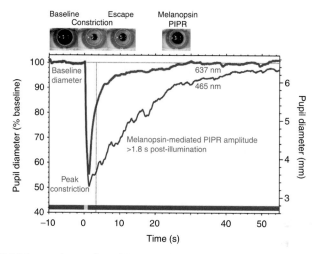

Figure 8 Melanopsin-mediated PLR under dark-adapted viewing conditions. Consensual pupillary light responses to 1 s pulses in Maxwellian view (35.6° diameter stimulus; 15.1 log quanta.cm^{-2}.s^{-1}). The melanopsin excitation of the stimulus was high (blue pupil trace; 465 nm) or low (red pupil trace; 637 nm). The PIPR constriction amplitude is larger and more sustained following offset of lights with higher melanopsin excitation (blue trace). The thick, bottom horizontal line represents the pre- and post-stimulus periods in the dark; the mark at time 0 represents the stimulus pulse.Data are for a representative healthy observer. Modified after Kelbsch et al. (2019).

Stimulus lights with peaks nearer to the λ_{max} of the melanopsin photopigment (e.g., λ_{max} = ~482 nm, cyanish/bluish appearing) produce higher melanopsin excitation (Figure 6) (Kelbsch et al. 2019). This PLR to onset of the narrow-band light includes an initial rapid pupil constriction dominated by the outer retina, with the cone and rod photoreceptors most sensitive to the stimulus wavelength driving the constriction (i.e., winner-takes-all) (McDougal and Gamlin 2010). Melanopsin contributes a slower, sustained constriction during presentation of stimulus light close to its peak spectral response, as evidenced from a single-case study of a blind person due to rod–cone degeneration (Gooley et al. 2012), but which is not evident in the PLR due to a greater relative response of the outer retinal photoreceptors to the stimulus. Following light offset, the PIPR amplitude increases with retinal irradiance, from a threshold level near 11.5 log quanta.cm^{-2}.s^{-1} to a half maximal response at ~13.5 log quanta.cm^{-2}.s^{-1} (Gamlin et al. 2007, Park et al. 2011, Adhikari et al. 2015b) with the sustained PIPR constriction extending for longer than a minute in daylight illumination (Adhikari et al. 2015b). Melanopsin as the primary driver of the PIPR was determined in macaque monkeys using pharmacological blockage of outer retina activity (Gamlin et al. 2007), and in trichromatic humans through estimation of the PIPR spectral response, estimated at λ_{max} of ~482 nm (Gamlin et al. 2007, Markwell et al. 2010, Adhikari et al. 2015b). The initial PIPR recovery at the very earliest pupil redilation times following light offset (<1.7 s post-stimulus) includes rhodopsin inputs (Adhikari et al. 2016a). While polymorphisms in the OPN4 alleles have been associated with lower pupil constriction amplitudes (OPN4 SNP I394 T (Higuchi et al. 2013)) and sleep disturbances (OPN4 SNP P10L (Roecklein et al. 2012)), there is no available evidence that these polymorphisms alter the spectral tuning of melanopsin, unlike the polymorphisms that can shift the peak sensitivities of the L- and M-cone opsins (Nathans et al. 1986, DeMarco et al. 1992). While a battery of psychophysical techniques need be applied to assess all photoreceptor contributions to human vision, the PLR can provide a direct, objective marker of rod, cone, and melanopsin function in a single recording (Markwell et al. 2010, Zele and Gamlin 2020).

Protocols for measuring and reporting the PIPR in research and clinical practice are described in the standards for pupillography (Kelbsch et al. 2019). The PIPR is typically measured in darkness to take advantage of melanopsin ipRGCs unique post-stimulus response properties (Gamlin et al. 2007). The techniques are now applied widely in ophthalmology and visual science in the detection and monitoring of eye diseases (for reviews, see Feigl and Zele 2014, La Morgia et al. 2018, Rukmini et al. 2019b) including glaucoma (Feigl et al. 2011a, Kankipati et al. 2011, Adhikari et al. 2016b), age-related macular degeneration (Maynard et al. 2015, 2017), diabetes (Feigl et al. 2011b, Park et al. 2017, Dumpala et al. 2019), and in neurological (Joyce et al. 2018, Chougule et al. 2019) and mood disorders (Roecklein et al. 2013, Laurenzo et al. 2016, Feigl et al. 2018) where melanopsin dysfunction may be evident before detectable changes in standard clinical ophthalmic markers. This melanopsin dysfunction can cause aberrant transmission of ambient light information signalled via ipRGC for photoentrainment (Feigl et al. 2018). Intrinsically photosensitive retinal ganglion cells are robust against aging until at least the seventh decade, as evidenced in pupillary (Kankipati et al. 2011, Adhikari et al. 2015a) and histological studies of human retina (Esquiva et al. 2017). Together with its reduced redundancy (Dacey et al. 2005), the melanopsin PIPR is a sensitive marker of neural dysfunction that is not confounded with age-related declines occurring in other retinogeniculate pathways (Feigl and Zele 2014). The melanopsin-mediated PIPR is retained in patients with outer retina dysfunction such as retinitis pigmentosa (Kardon et al. 2009, Markwell et al. 2010) and in optic nerve diseases including Leber hereditary optic neuropathy

(Kawasaki et al. 2010, Moura et al. 2013) and Leber congenital amaurosis (Collison et al. 2015) and is independent of refractive error (Adhikari et al. 2016b, Ostrin 2018, Rukmini et al. 2019a). The PIPR amplitude is stable during daylight hours (Zele et al. 2011, Münch et al. 2012). Spontaneous pupil movements (pupillary unrest) can be used to index sleepiness (Lüdtke et al. 1998) after accounting for the dual interaction of homeostatic and circadian processes (Daguet et al. 2019). It is also possible to create an objective map of retinal function to pupillary responses measured in focal areas across the visual field (Carle, James et al. 2011, Kelbsch et al. 2020).

6 Melanopsin-Driven Light Adaptation Modulates Rod- and Cone-Mediated Functions

While ipRGCs project to many brain centres, they also play an important role in regulating the intra-retinal signals that underpin visual sensation and perception. The mechanisms by which melanopsin ipRGCs regulate retinal function appear to be through chemical and electrical synapses within the retina. Retrograde synaptic connections linking ipRGCs and dopaminergic amacrine cells have been shown to play a key role in retinal light adaptation (Viney et al. 2007, Zhang et al. 2008, 2012, Prigge et al. 2016, Zhao et al. 2017, Munteanu et al. 2018). Melanopsin ipRGCs are also coupled to other retinal cell types via GJs, providing an additional mechanism by which they may modulate visual signalling (Sekaran et al. 2003). Different melanopsin subtypes may play different roles in visual processing. For example, mouse studies reveal that M4 ipRGCs contribute to contrast sensitivity (Estevez et al. 2012, Schmidt et al. 2014), and recently, a subtype of M5 ipRGC has been shown to be coupled to inhibitory amacrine cells that express corticotrophin-releasing hormone (CRH) to modulate the function of other retinal ganglion cells (Pottackal et al. 2021).

The melanopsin excitation of light can directly influence rod- and cone-mediated visual functions. A determination of the effects of melanopsin–rhodopsin interactions are being actively investigated. Unique white perception, the equilibrium point of the opponent processes for colour vision, can be shifted with changes in the melanopsin excitation (Cao et al. 2018). An implication is that the CIE standard observer colour matching functions, the basis of modern colorimetry, may depend on the melanopsin excitation of their initial measurement conditions (Barrionuevo et al. 2022). Analysis of natural scene images reveals that melanopsin contributes to the putative red-green (parvocellular) and blue-yellow (koniocellular) colour opponent pathways, in addition to the luminance (magnocellular) pathway (Barrionuevo and Cao 2014). When melanopsin excitation is increased, and without altering the mean photopic luminance, contrast discrimination improves for lights modulated along each of the cardinal cone directions (Zele et al. 2019b). This contrast enhancement in humans has a parallel in mice wherein visual contrast sensitivity is higher in wild-type than in melanopsin-deficient transgenic lines (Schmidt et al. 2014). A higher melanopsin excitation also increases the spatial tuning of mouse dLGN neurons from long pass to band pass (Allen et al. 2014).

It is through adaptation processes that visual contrast sensitivity and spatial and temporal resolution are optimized across a 10-log unit range of illumination when individual cells are restricted to a narrower dynamic range of 2–3 log units (MacLeod 1978, Shapley and Enroth-Cugell 1984, Hood 1998). The first site of adaptation occurs at the photoreceptor. Transduction of light into sensory neural signals leads to a conformational change in the photopigments that initiates a recovery process that is 3.4× slower in humans for the melanopsin photopigment than the cone-opsins, and 1.2× faster than rhodopsin (Pant et al. 2021). The partial resistance of melanopsin to pigment bleaching is likely due to its unique chromophore (Sexton et al. 2012, Emanuel and Do 2015) and the displacement of ipRGCs from the retinal pigment epithelium (Tu et al. 2006, Zhao et al. 2016). Second-site adaptation processes at post-receptoral retinal and cortical sites implement fast and slow gain controls to fine tune contrast sensitivity. In humans, Weberian adaptation supports achromatic contrast invariance (delta L/L = constant) (Aguilar and Stiles 1954) and low temporal frequency behaviour (de Lange 1954, Kelly 1961), but such invariance is not evident for visual responses mediated via the colour-opponent chromatic pathways (Swanson et al. 1987, Smith et al. 2008). The sub-Weber adaptation response of the afferent pupil light reflex (Barrionuevo and Cao 2016) indicates that melanopsin pathways can drive adaptive changes in neuronal circuits separately from the Weber adaptation controlled by the magnocellular pathway (Smith et al. 2008). Cone-mediated visual contrast response functions (Chen et al. 2000) follow different patterns than with melanopsin-directed lights, such that the melanopsin pathway can modulate the gain of the cone pathways (Zele et al. 2019b). Higher melanopsin activations also modulate the gain of mice retinal ganglion cells to improve information transfer rates (Milosavljevic et al. 2018). Melanopsin-driven adaptation processes can optimize the connectivity and response properties of local retinal neuronal networks in reaction to incoming light signals through feedforward and feedback networks connecting the intraretinal melanopsin pathway with the rod and cone photoreceptors (Lee et al. 2004, Zhang et al. 2008, Grünert et al. 2011, Newkirk et al. 2013, Reifler et al. 2015). For example, the steady-state white noise electroretinogram (wnERG) as a measure of melanopsin- or cone-initiated photoresponses in humans has detected interference between these outer and inner retinal signal generators, leading to a reduction in the electroretinogram (ERG) amplitude when simultaneously activated (Adhikari et al. 2019b). The flash ERG as a measure of outer retinal function also shows a light-dependent adaption response matching the spectral response properties of melanopsin (Hankins and Lucas 2002). The diurnal variation of the cone ERG in mice show that these changes are abolished in mice lacking melanopsin, suggesting that ipRGC responses may play a role in optimizing visual function to the time of day (Barnard et al. 2006). Along with its visual and non-visual responses to light, there is much to be discovered about how the melanopsin pathway interacts with and supports the activity and behaviour of the retina and downstream cortical networks, to optimize performance of rod- and cone-mediated visual functions with changes in light adaptation.

7 Spatio-Temporal Response Properties of Melanopsin Photoreception

A hallmark of melanopsin photoreception is their sluggish temporal kinetics, kinetics that can be orders of magnitude slower than that of the canonical image-forming pathways. In non-human primates, melanopsin cells with their sustained responses have lower temporal fidelity (Dacey et al. 2005) than the midget (critical flicker frequency, CFF ~100 Hz), parasol (CFF ~100 Hz) (Smith et al. 2008), and small bistratified retinal ganglion cells (CFF ~80 Hz) (Crook et al. 2009) that form the early physiologic pathway for image-forming vision. Human visual temporal contrast sensitivity mediated via the melanopsin pathway is low pass, with a resolution limit near ~5 Hz (Zele et al. 2018c). Compared to the band-pass, achromatic response of the cone pathway wherein the CFF increases linearly with logarithmic changes in luminance according to the Ferry–Porter law, the melanopsin-mediated CFF is independent of illumination level (200–5000 Td) (Zele et al. 2018c) and lower than for achromatic (CFF >60 Hz), red-green (~16 Hz) (Swanson et al. 1987), or blue-yellow chromatic modulations (~20 Hz) (Zele et al. 2018c). Visual reaction times are also longer to melanopsin- than cone-directed stimuli (Gnyawali et al. 2022) while contrast sensitivities depend on the melanopic response to light; melanopsin stimulation facilitates (improves) the temporal contrast sensitivity of the cone pathway while rod pathway temporal contrast sensitivity can be facilitated or inhibited depending on the stimulus temporal frequency (Uprety et al. 2022).

The flicker PLR (fPLR) mediated via ipRGCs in macaques (Ostrin et al. 2018) and humans (Gooley et al. 2012) is low pass, but with a cut-off near ~8 Hz (Stark and Sherman 1957, Clarke et al. 2003, Joyce et al. 2015, Adhikari et al. 2019a), higher than for melanopsin-mediated vision due to extrinsic rod and cone inputs to ipRGCs. These extrinsic inputs linearly summate with the intrinsic melanopsin signals (Barrionuevo et al. 2014). The dominant extrinsic contributions to pupil constriction (McDougal and Gamlin 2010) have a similar critical duration (75–100 ms) to that for image-forming visual processes (Webster 1969), although melanopsin signalling delays the time to peak constriction (Joyce et al. 2015). Outer retinal temporal summation is important for rapidly controlling pupil diameter in response to short timescale fluctuations in illumination and may occur at two potential sites, one that is presynaptic to the extrinsic photoreceptor input to ipRGCs (Barrionuevo et al. 2018), and another within the pupil control pathway if ipRGCs have differential temporal tuning to the extrinsic and intrinsic signals (Joyce et al. 2015). As for the PIPR following offset of an incremental stimulus pulse, the intrinsic melanopsin photoresponse manifests within the fPLR as a suppression of its peak-to-trough amplitude at high irradiances (Feigl and Zele 2014, Joyce et al. 2015), consistent with an increase in the relative melanopsin:rhodopsin weighting in ipRGCs with transitions between scotopic and photopic lighting (Adhikari et al. 2019a).

The topology of photoreceptors and ganglion cells varies across the retina, with implications for spatial vision. In human and macaque retina, the spatial resolution of the melanopsin pathway is constrained by its giant dendritic field sizes, with ipRGC diameters ranging from 350 μm in the parafovea to 1200 μm in peripheral retina (Dacey et al. 2005, Liao et al. 2016, Nasir-Ahmad et al. 2017). Compared to the cone pathways, ipRGC dendritic field diameters are ~6.7–87.5× larger than midget ganglion cells projections to the parvocellular layers of LGN, ~3.0–11.6× larger than parasol cells in the magnocellular pathway, and ~3.0–17.5× larger than small bi-stratified cells in the koniocellular pathway. Hence, the melanopsin pathway in humans can provide a coarse spatial representation of images up to a resolution limit at about 0.8 cycles per degree (c/°) in the superotemporal visual space (Allen et al. 2019b). Similarly, rudimentary spatial vision is retained in mice that have defective rod–cone transduction but intact melanopsin transduction (Ecker et al. 2010, Brown et al. 2012). Further mapping across the visual field is required to determine how human spatial vision is dependent on variations in ipRGC topography, melanopsin photopigment density and the large photoreceptive net ipRGCs form across the retina. With their smaller receptive fields, cone-mediated vision subserves a higher spatial resolution limit of ~60 c/° (Campbell and Green 1965). For middle and longer wavelength interference patterns detected by the L- and M-cones, spatial resolution is limited by the cone diameter whereas spatial detection limits are set by the ganglion cell spacing (Thibos et al. 1987, Anderson et al. 2002, Zhu et al. 2016). For short wavelength interference patterns, detection is better than resolution, possibly limited by S-cone spacing, and lower than for L- and M-cones

(Metha and Lennie 2001, Zhu et al. 2016). The spatial resolution limits of rod-mediated vision are a further 1-log unit lower, with integration areas 16 times greater than for cone vision to increase sensitivity in low photon conditions (Zele and Cao 2015). As an irradiance detector, the non-image-forming pupil control pathway does not require high spatial resolution (Crawford 1936, Stanley and Davies 1995) and the melanopsin-driven PIPR amplitudes are determined by the corneal flux density of a stimulus that is the product of the stimulus energy and its area (Park and McAnany 2015, Joyce et al. 2016b). The melanopsin-driven PIPRs in the peripheral retina are lower in amplitude than in the central retina, in opposition to the outer retina driven constriction amplitude that does not exhibit a retinal eccentricity dependent change in amplitude (Joyce et al. 2016b). This points to a difference in the spatial tuning characteristics of the extrinsic (rod/ cone) and intrinsic (melanopsin) mediated pathways across the retina, as well as in their temporal tuning (Joyce et al. 2015). In mice, melanopsin activation can alter the spatial and temporal feature selectivity of visual circuits (Allen et al. 2014) and enhance the encoding of spatial patterns (Allen et al. 2017). On the other hand, contrast sensitivity is reduced in melanopsin null mice, with no change in their acuity (Schmidt et al. 2014). Distinctions in spike amplitude, frequency, and decay of different ipRGC subtypes, as evident in mouse models (Schmidt and Kofuji 2009, Ecker et al. 2010, Zhao et al. 2014), are the encryption required for various brain regions (e.g., OPN, SCN, LGN, V1) to distinguish the temporal and spatial differences in the extrinsic and intrinsic signals encoded in the same ipRGC axons (Joyce et al. 2015, 2016b). Understanding the functional consequences of the unique anatomical and physiological bounds of the ipRGC pathway will help define how human spatial, temporal, and colour vision is controlled and supported during illumination changes through the morphological properties of the retinal networks driven by melanopsin.

8 Melanopsin-Expressing ipRGCs Drive an Independent Dimension of Conscious Visual Perception in Humans

In primates, ipRGCs project to central brain regions involved in the processing of visual information, such as the dLGN and SC (Figure 5) (Dacey et al. 2005, Hannibal et al. 2014). Following the development of new optical instrumentation and psychophysical methodologies, an accumulation of evidence now points to a role for melanopsin as the fifth photoreceptor class capable of delivering information for human visual perception. Both the inner and outer stratifying melanopsin cells in macaque retina project to the dLGN to relay inputs to the primary visual cortex (Liao et al. 2016) for conscious image-forming vision. Brightness magnitude estimates with increasing light level follow a power function that is approximately linear (versus log luminance) at high photopic levels (Stevens and Stevens 1963, Barlow and Verrillo 1976, Mansfield 1976). It is the intrinsic melanopsin photon counting response property that delivers the time-average signal of the ambient lighting required to support the perceptual quality of brightness (Dacey et al. 2005). By comparison, canonical retinal ganglion cells with their centre-surround configuration are optimized for signalling contrast (Kuffler 1953), and by nature, remove information about the external light level. Consequently, psychophysical discrimination experiments in trichromats in photopic lighting show that cone metamers with a higher melanopsin excitation appear brighter than comparison metamers with lower melanopsin excitation (Brown et al. 2012, Besenecker and Bullough 2016, Zele et al. 2018a, Yamakawa et al. 2019, DeLawyer et al. 2020). In the spectral region where melanopsin has highest sensitivity, a blind person with outer retinal rod and cone degeneration reportedly experienced a brightness percept with preserved circadian entrainment and pupillary light responses (Zaidi et al. 2007). It is, however, the combined response of melanopsin and the conventional retinogeniculate visual pathways that are required to support brightness perception in trichromats (Zele et al. 2018a, 2020b) with some models proposing a role for S-cones (Bullough (2018) but see Zele et al. (2018b)). In scotopic lighting, brightness information is entirely signalled by rhodopsin activation, likely through the magnocellular pathway and extrinsic inputs to ipRGCs (Zele et al. 2020b), the former includes a dominant rod weighting (Lee et al. 1997). An independent melanopsin contribution to brightness estimation is first evident in mesopic illumination, with the less sensitive rod signals overshadowed by cone inputs to the magnocellular pathway (Zele et al. 2020b) that forms the substrate for cone photometric luminance (Lennie et al. 1993). When the illumination reaches levels sufficiently high to cause light aversion, this photophobic spectral response matches the action spectrums of the melanopsin and cone-luminance pathways, with light-sensitive migraineurs experiencing melanopsin hypersensitivity (Zele et al. 2020a).

The intrinsic melanopsin visual response to a spatially uniform, photoreceptor-directed incremental pulse requires more than $10\times$ higher contrast than for detection of stimuli mediated via the putative red-green pathway (inferred +L-M cone opponent), and with lower sensitivity than to stimulus transitions along the blue-yellow (inferred S-cone opponent pathway) or achromatic dimension (inferred non-opponent pathway) (Zele et al. 2018c). The conscious melanopsin-mediated visual percept to very high stimulus levels (e.g., 400%) evokes a measurable fMRI activation change in the primary visual cortex (Spitschan et al. 2017). Psychophysically measured melanopsin photoreception thresholds require lower stimulus contrasts (Horiguchi et al. 2013, Cao et al.

2015, Zele et al. 2018c, 2019b, Allen et al. 2019b) than is necessary to elicit a response in single-cell recordings of the mouse dLGN to melanopsin-directed stimuli (Allen et al. 2017). On the other hand, melanopsin-expressing ipRGCs in mice are capable of single photon responses of a larger scale than rods (Do et al. 2009), yet at the absolute threshold of human vision (Hecht et al. 1942), detection is driven entirely by the scotopic rod pathway with an action spectrum matching the rhodopsin photopigment (Dey et al. 2021). The single-cell and systems level roles of melanopsin can therefore be functionally different. Melanopsin contributions to human contrast processing first become manifest in intermediate mesopic illumination levels (~200 Td) when all five photoreceptors provide functional input to human visual perception (Zele et al. 2019b). Both the sparseness of ipRGCs (Dacey et al. 2005) and the low membrane density of melanopsin (Do et al. 2009) are factors driving its low contrast sensitivity. Rod- and cone-mediated vision is exquisitely sensitive to changes in the spatio-temporal properties of the light across the visual field and with variation illumination level (Hess et al. 1990, Buck 2003, Makous 2003, Reeves 2003), with many of these factors still untested for the melanopsin pathway. Beyond the fundamental knowledge gained through study of melanopsin contributions to human vision, and its interaction with the rod and cone pathways to drive visual function, there will be new developments in understanding of the role of melanopsin dysfunction in the pathomechanisms of ophthalmic and neurological disease.

The visual percepts associated with melanopsin-directed stimulation include a change in colour and brightness, the latter sometimes with no apparent change in chromaticity. Earlier reports for rod-mediated colour perception acknowledged that in the dark-adapted eye with a central scotoma, there is a certain range of fluctuations as to its perceptual quality (Nagel 1924), with a rod hue sensation appearing bluish-green of little saturation (Nagel 1924, Buck 2003, Pokorny et al. 2006, Stabell and Stabell 2009). If the melanopsin colour percept was fully determined by its colour opponent L+M-ON and S-OFF response property in the retina, it is expected to include a component greenish/blueish-yellowish colouration (Cao et al. 2018). Colour appearance and naming is, however, complexly dependent on the viewing context and its neural representation is contingent on post-receptoral transformations at multiple sites within retina and cortex (Shevell and Kingdom 2007). By restricting verbal reports to the basic hues, melanopsin-directed lights reportedly appear more greenish and yellowish (Cao et al. 2018). With unrestricted subjective colour naming, subjects self-report that melanopsin excitation gives rise to a diffuse visual percepts that range from yellow-orange or greenish (Spitschan et al. 2017) to a bluish-cyanish or orangish appearance (Zele et al. 2019b). Objective colour matching of melanopsin-directed stimuli measured under conditions designed to eliminate penumbral cone intrusions returns a colour match that mirrors the L+M-ON and S-OFF response property (Zele et al. 2018c). Together this highlights that the commonality of between-observer objective colour matches can co-exist with different subjective colour appearances.

9 Circadian Rhythms and ipRGCs

Circadian rhythms are a fundamental process that occurs in nearly all living organisms. These rhythms are endogenous, near-24-hour oscillations that are self-sustaining and temperature-compensated (Mistlberger and Rusak 2005). Circadian rhythms are critical to establish daily cycles of physiology and behaviour that are predictive of changes in the environment driven by the 24-hour geophysical day. The external 24-hour day in most organisms is experienced through a daily cycle of light and dark driven by the rising and setting of the sun. In humans, as with all mammals, most circadian rhythms derive from a single neural locus, the SCN (Figure 5) (Moore and Lenn 1972, Stephan and Zucker 1972). The SCN are a dense pair of nuclei, each consisting of about 10,000 highly interconnected neurons, located at the base of the third ventricle and directly above the optic chiasm (Welsh et al. 2010). The SCN have a singular output as a pacemaker and help to synchronize many parts of the brain and body to both each other and the outside world. Without adequate light input to the SCN, the clock would 'free run' at its intrinsic non-24-hour pace (n. b., in humans, the average period length of the clock is 24.2 hours (Czeisler et al. 1999)). Under such conditions, the internal clock would slowly become misaligned (desynchronized) with the outside world and cycle through periods of synchronization and desynchronization based on the length of this internal period and the external day cycle. As an example, an individual with a circadian period length of 24.5 hours who had no light input to the clock would have their internal clock move one time zone every two days relative to the outside world, a permanent state of going into and out of jet lag.

Mammalian SCN are not directly photosensitive. Some circadian clocks in the other vertebrate classes such as birds, reptiles, fish, or amphibians have direct co-localization between light-sensing proteins and the clock (e.g., chicken pinealocytes (Deguchi 1981)). Other circadian clocks in non-mammalian vertebrates are not directly photosensitive, but receive light input from non-retinal (deep brain) photoreceptors (e.g., lizard SCN (Underwood 1973, Tosini et al. 2001)). Mammals do not have evidence of deep brain photoreceptors (Underwood and Groos 1982); direct exposure of the brain to light in enucleated rodents does not evoke circadian responses to light

(Groos and van der Kooy 1981). As the mammalian SCN is neither directly light sensitive nor are there deep brain photoreceptors to send it photic information, retinal input is necessary to synchronize the internal clock with the outside world.

The retinohypothalamic tract (RHT) is a monosynaptic neural pathway from the retina to the SCN in mammals (Moore 1995). It is made of a small fraction of the total number of retinal ganglion cells, likely about 1% (Moore et al. 1995). Evidence for the RHT as a bundle independent of the optic tract comes from both lesion (Johnson et al. 1998) and tract-tracing studies (Moore and Lenn 1972, Pickard 1980, Sadun et al. 1984, Dai et al. 1998). The RHT arises from a subset of ganglion cells with large dendritic and receptive fields originally identified as being type-W or type-III ganglion cells (Moore et al. 1995, Provencio et al. 1998a). It was later determined that the RHT arises from a molecularly distinguishable subset of retinal ganglion cells that express melanopsin (Provencio et al. 1998b, 2000). More specifically, the SCN are primarily innervated by a portion of the RHT that arises from the M1 subtype of ipRGC that lack expression of Brn3b SCN (Chen et al. 2011, Fernandez et al. 2016).

The ipRGCs that make up the RHT are both directly photosensitive, due to the ability of melanopsin to convert an electromagnetic signal into an electro-chemical signal, and receive input from rods and cones (Mure 2021). The exact manner in which the melanopsin, rod, and cone signals are integrated by the ipRGCs that convey photic information to the SCN is not well understood. Evidence from rodents indicates that all three likely play a role in providing light information to the circadian clock (Berson et al. 2002, Ruby et al. 2002, Altimus et al. 2010, Lall et al. 2010, Walmsley et al. 2015), and human SCN responses are suppressed by narrowband light stimuli that range the visible spectrum (blue, green, and orange lights), though not for violet light, which entails relatively greater S-cone excitation (Schoonderwoerd et al. 2022). Human studies attempting to parse out photoreceptor contributions to circadian function are now emerging: Blind individuals lacking an outer retina (and so rods and cones) are still able to entrain to the solar day and demonstrate visual perceptions that correspond to the action spectrum of melanopsin (Zaidi et al. 2007). Studies of S-cone circuit connectomics (Patterson et al. 2020), electro-physiology (Dacey et al. 2005), and pupillary responses (Spitschan et al. 2014, Cao et al. 2015) indicate that S-cone signals may be opponent to melanopsin signal output. Results are mixed when explored in a circadian context, however; one study demonstrated no effect of S-cones in suppressing the circadian hormone melatonin over 2 hours of stimulation in participants with undilated (natural) pupils (Spitschan et al. 2019), while another demonstrated a large effect (half as strong as that of the melanopsin signal itself) in suppressing melatonin for brief 30 min durations in participants with dilated pupils (Brown et al. 2021).

The SCN use information about the external light-dark cycle to set the time (phase) and pace (period) of the circadian clock. The impact of light on the circadian clock is dependent on the circadian time at which the light is applied. This relationship between the timing of light exposure and subsequent responses to light is known as a 'phase response curve' (Johnson 1990, Khalsa et al. 2003). In individuals who are normally entrained (synchronized) to the 24-hour day, light in the evening and early night will cause delays in circadian timing. In other words, light will temporarily slow down the clock and events the next day will be shifted to a later time. For example, if the peak of cortisol, which is under circadian control, were to occur at 6 a.m. today, following an evening light exposure, it might occur at 7 a.m. the next day. Light at the end of the night and early morning will cause advances in circadian timing. In other words, light will temporarily speed up the clock and events the next day will be shifted to an earlier time. Light during the daytime has a comparatively less effect on the timing of the clock (St Hilaire et al. 2012), but is important because it can mitigate the impact of evening light exposure (Chang et al. 2011). Thus, greater amounts of light exposure during the daytime can reduce the circadian response to evening light, while circadian responses to morning light are left relatively unaffected when preceded by a night of sleep in darkness (Zeitzer et al. 2011a).

Individuals with erratic schedules or working night shifts are likely to have a different relationship between the timing of sleep and circadian time. As such, while there is a phase response curve in these individuals as well, the position of this phase response curve relative to the timing of sleep, such as described earlier, is less predictable (Stone et al. 2019). The timing of sleep is controlled at a biological level by two processes, the circadian clock and a homeostatic process (Borbély 1982, Dijk and Czeisler 1994). The homeostatic control of sleep is through an unknown neural locus and represents an appetitive process – the more you sleep, the less sleep you need, and the longer you stay awake, the more sleep you need. In humans, the circadian clock provides a maximal drive for wake in what is typically the late evening hours and a maximal drive for sleep near the end of the normal sleep period. The circadian clock counterbalances the increased homeostatic drive for sleep at the end of the day and the increased homeostatic drive for wake at the end of the sleep period, thereby consolidating both the wake and sleep periods. The timing of these circadian drives is mostly independent of actual sleep behaviour as they are set by the circadian clock and, therefore, the timing of light exposure. Individuals with erratic sleep schedules (erratic light exposure), shift workers (displaced and inconsistent light exposure), and travellers (displaced light exposure) will each have a disruption in the relative position between the circadian clock, homeo-static sleep pressure, and desired sleep timing, resulting in an inability to fall asleep, stay asleep, or stay awake. This type of erratic exposure to light can also cause a decrease in the amplitude of the circadian clock (Jewett et al. 1994), leading to downstream reduction in the influence of the SCN on behaviours such as sleep timing.

In addition to the timing of the light, the intensity of the light can have a significant impact on the magnitude of the circadian response to light. This relationship is known as a 'dose response curve' or 'irradiance response curve' (Figure 1) (Zeitzer et al. 2000). In humans, the dose response relationship between light intensity and subsequent circadian responses to light follows a sigmoidal relationship such that low intensities of light generate relatively little change in phase (lower asymptote), very high intensities of light generate maximal change in phase (upper asymptote), and increasing light intensities between these two extremes logarithmically results in a linear increase in phase change (Zeitzer et al. 2000, 2005). Under laboratory conditions in which the system is sensitized by multi-day exposure to dim light, this logarithmic rise occurs in the range of normal room light. It is likely that under real-world conditions, this logarithmic rise is shifted to higher intensities for evening exposure to light but would remain in the room light range for morning expos-ure to light when preceded by a night of sleep in darkness. Individual differ-ences appear to be an important factor in circadian study of light sensitivity; under laboratory-controlled conditions, melatonin suppression by light can vary 50-fold between individuals (Phillips et al. 2019). Whether these differences in light sensitivity originate in ipRGCs or elsewhere in the circadian pathway remains unknown (Chellappa 2020).

The length of exposure to light is another factor that can modulate the impact of light on circadian timing. In general, there are diminishing returns for extended exposure to light, with exposure times in the minutes being much more potent in terms of the amount of shift generated per photon of light exposure (Rimmer et al. 2000, Chang et al. 2012, Rahman et al. 2017a). Duration of exposure, however, can be manipulated to induce illusions in the circadian system, in which the circadian system responds to light that is not present. The ipRGC projections to the SCN remain depolarized for several minutes following light offset (Berson et al. 2002). In essence, these cells continue to respond to a light stimulation that is no longer present, but with a post-stimulus spike-frequency related to the number of stimulus photons (Dacey et al. 2005). This electrophysiologic phenomenon is functionally relevant as when a train of millisecond-length light pulses are strung together with 60 seconds of darkness interspersed between the pulses, the circadian system responds as if it had been exposed to an equiluminant continuous light pulse (Zeitzer et al. 2011b). When the light pulses are separated by 8 seconds of interspersed darkness, the response of the circadian system is two to three fold greater than with an equiluminant continuous light pulse (Najjar and Zeitzer 2016). The enhanced response of the circadian system is likely due to these pulses of light acting extrinsically through cones (Wong and Fernandez 2021).

10 The Non-image-Forming Pathways Set Arousal and Cognition

It has been widely assumed that due to increased responses to blue (~460 nm) compared with green/yellow stimuli (~555 nm), the melanopsin ipRGC system may be critically involved in alerting responses to light. Such stimulus lights are not, however, optimally designed to separate the relative contributions of the inner and outer retinal inputs to these responses. However, these supposed mechanisms are largely based upon analogy to other non-visual effects of light such as circadian entrainment. The relative strengths of photoreceptor inputs and the neural circuits mediating the effects of light on alertness are yet to be fully elucidated.

Given our mastery over electric lighting technology and its ubiquity in society, there has been immense interest in how broadband (white or whitish) lighting such as we use indoors can drive subjective alertness as well as objective performance and brain physiology. Mechanistically, ipRGCs project to areas involved in alerting, including the anterior hypothalamus, LHb, MA, and SPZ (Hattar et al. 2006, LeGates et al. 2014), and light modulates the sympathetic nervous system though projections from the SCN to the paraventricular nuclei of the hypothalamus. People often have an intuitive idea of what it means to feel alert (or not), yet alertness remains hard to define (Oken et al. 2006). In psychological approaches, alertness often refers to vigilance and the ability to maintain sustained attention and cognitive performance (Shapiro et al. 2006), while sleep-wake studies often simply define alertness as the opposite of sleep or a reduced sleep need (Aston-Jones 2005, Cajochen 2007). Studies of the alerting effect of light can thus use a variety of measures to probe alertness.

The intensity of white light during the biological night has a dose-dependent effect on alertness where participants transition between sleepy and alert between ~70 and ~200 lux (Cajochen et al. 2000). This range is surprisingly precise given its derivation from self-reported sleepiness, eye movements, and electroencephalography (EEG) spectral manifestations of alertness. A systematic review by Souman et al. (2017) identified 38 studies of white light intensity spanning some 47 separate experimental cohorts. These studies evaluated the effect of 'dim' versus 'bright' light, which varied considerably by study (dim minimum = ~0.01 lux, maximum = ~1,411 lux, median = ~170 lux; bright minimum = ~100 lux, maximum = ~10,000 lux, median = ~2,250 lux). Of these, approximately two-thirds of studies reported increases in alertness with bright light compared to dim light, while approximately a third reported no effect or a decrease in alertness. These conflicting results may be because the dim light control condition in some studies was ~100 lux or greater, and so may actually be alerting. Of the studies reported in Souman et al. (2017), 6 of 15 studies that reported no effect involved dim light conditions ≥100 lux (Dollins et al. 1993, Leproult et al. 1997, Iskra-Golec et al. 2000, O'Brien and O'Connor 2000, Crasson and Legros 2005, Borisuit et al. 2015). A further three studies that did report dim light effects at one time of exposure reported no effect at other times (Teixeira et al. 2013, Smolders and de Kort 2014, Huiberts et al. 2015), suggesting that light intensity was approximately at threshold for alertness. It is less clear how these findings apply to performance because some studies report positive effects on psychomotor vigilance or letter-digit substitution tests of cognition (Phipps-Nelson et al. 2003, Smolders et al. 2012), but others report negative effects (Iskra-Golec et al. 2000). The relation between subjective alertness and performance may not be direct and is further confounded, sleepiness may not always translate to worsened vigilance and attention, while the effects may be task-dependent.

Studies have also evaluated narrowband (monochromatic) lights because, when carefully selected, they can bias activation towards the desired photoreceptor class(es) (e.g., the melanopsin pathway) relative to other classes but with the restriction that they differentially activate more than one photoreceptor class (except in scotopic lighting) and therefore multiple pathways. Souman et al. (2017) also evaluated studies that used ~440 to ~555 nm narrowband (blueish to greenish) lights to manipulate alertness and performance. Alertness was increased by these lights in four studies, decreased in one, and had no effect in nine. Eight of these studies also evaluated performance but only five found positive effects. A common specification of commercial white light is its CCT along the Planckian (black body) locus, where lower values appear reddish and higher values bluish white; typical room lighting values range from 2,600°K (warm lighting) to 6,500 °K (cool lighting). With these manipulations to lights, findings are again mixed. Of three studies of performance (Souman et al. 2017), only one found positive effects (Chellappa et al. 2011). If blue light is filtered out of the spectrum (expected to reduce melanopsin drive, but also altering the excitations of the rod and cone photoreceptors), studies are again mixed: of four studies of performance, two found effects on performance when reducing short wavelength content (Rahman et al. 2011, 2013). An important consideration is that these lighting manipulations can translate into relatively small shifts along the dose response curves that may be readily eclipsed by inter- or intra individual differences due to biological variability or lifestyle factors (Phillips et al. 2019). Thus, very large sample sizes would be needed to reliably detect such small effect sizes.

While the subjective data are largely inconclusive, more objective measures of alertness such as EEG provide a window into happenings at the neurophysiological level. Studies consistently report effects of white light on EEG measures including decreased theta (θ, 5–8 Hz) and alpha (α, 9–13 Hz) frequencies (Cajochen et al. 2000, Daurat et al. 2000, Lavoie et al. 2003), increased beta (β, 14–30 Hz) power (Badia et al. 1991, Lavoie et al. 2003), and reduced slow eye movements (Cajochen et al. 2000). Monochromatic light exposures also decrease theta frequencies (Lockley et al. 2006, Phipps-Nelson et al. 2009, Sahin and Figueiro 2013) and suppress the delta (δ, 0.5–4 Hz) frequencies associated with increasing sleep drive (Lockley et al. 2006, Münch et al. 2006, Phipps-Nelson et al. 2009, Rahman et al. 2014). In contrast to white light, the alpha frequencies increase in response to blue versus green light (Lockley et al. 2006, Rahman et al. 2014) but reductions in alpha frequencies have also been described in response to both blue and red stimuli, with no wavelength-dependent effects (Figueiro et al. 2009, Sahin and Figueiro 2013, Okamoto et al. 2014). White light with higher CCTs tend to decrease delta (Cajochen et al. 2011, Chellappa et al. 2013) and theta frequencies (Cajochen et al. 2011, Sahin et al. 2014). Consistent with these findings, reduced blue light content results in increases in both delta and theta frequencies (Rahman et al. 2017b). Thus, objective EEG measures provide good evidence of light-dependent effects on EEG-defined alertness, consistent with the greater effects of blue versus green light on plasma melatonin suppression, subjective sleepiness, and reaction time.

There have been relatively fewer brain imaging studies on alertness. During the night, bright light (8,000 lux) increases activation levels in the striate cortex, extrastriate cortex, and intraparietal sulcus, areas involved visual and auditory attention (Perrin et al. 2004). Blood flow was decreased at stimulus offset in hypothalamic areas, although it is unclear if this reflects the SCN or related hypothalamic nuclei due to the resolution constraints of imaging. During the day, bright white light (>7,000 lux) combined with an oddball auditory task revealed that increases in subjective alertness associate with increasing activation of the posterior thalamus, and that dynamic changes in cortical activity cease rapidly at stimulus offset. These studies also suggest that subcortical structures associated with alertness are activated prior to widespread cortical activation (Vandewalle et al. 2006). Monochromatic light also has been evaluated, comparing morning light exposure to 13.5 log quanta.cm^{-2}.s^{-1} of either blue (470 nm) or green (550 nm) light (18 minute exposure) during an auditory working memory task. Wavelength-dependent effects on brain regions were found in areas associated with executive function (frontal and parietal cortex, insula and thalamus) were involved in these responses, but only during the stimulus presentation. Blue light enhanced responses/prevented the decline observed during green light stimuli (Vandewalle et al. 2007a). Follow-up studies used violetish (430 nm), blueish (473 nm), and greenish (527 nm) stimuli (13 log quanta.cm^{-2}.s^{-1}). Blueish light resulted in increased activation of thalamus, hippocampus, and amygdala compared with greenish light and an increase in activity in the middle frontal gyrus, thalamus and the brainstem compared to violetish light (Vandewalle et al. 2007b). Consistent effects on frontal cortex were observed when applying 30 minutes of exposure to bright blueish (479 nm, 14.7–15.5 log quanta.cm^{-2}.s^{-1}) and amberish (578 nm, 14.0– 15.0 log quanta.cm^{-2}.s^{-1}) lights. Blueish light increased performance on an N-back task, and increased activation in executive function areas associated with the dorsolateral and ventrolateral prefrontal cortices (Alkozei et al. 2016). While not directly separating the melanopsin and cone contributions, these findings are consistent with the known ipRGC projections such as links between the SCN and wake-promoting nuclei of the brain and projections to the thalamus and amygdala (Figure 5). There are also interindividual effects that temper these responses to light. The effects of blue light on cortical activation are reduced in ageing, even when controlling for reduced lens transmittance (brunescence) and pupil size (senile miosis) with increasing age (Daneault et al. 2014). Prior light exposure history affects working memory tasks under greenish light (515 nm) where prior light exposure increased prefrontal and pulvinar responses follow- ing amber (589 nm) rather than blue (462 nm) light. The authors suggest that this may be due to prior light exposure resulting in greater photoconversion of melanopsin to its active state (Chellappa et al. 2014), but there is minimal evidence of this when studied in vivo (Lucas et al. 2014).

Because light can be efficacious in modulating arousal and cognition, more targeted modulations of the photoreceptor pathways have been explored in applied contexts using devices that could conveivably be integrated into real- world environs. When viewing movies in the biological evening on a novel five- primary visual display, both subjective sleepiness and melatonin expression were reduced by high melanopsin/rod stimulation compared to low melanopsin/ rod stimulation (Allen et al. 2018). When deployed as room lighting, metameric daytime lights but with varying levels of melanopsin stimulation modulated the pupil light reflex in a dose- and illuminance-dependent manner, but modulated objective sleepiness at low (100 lux) illuminance only (de Zeeuw et al. 2019). Indeed, while differences in cognitive functions were seen when participants were exposed to different ~4,000 K 100 lux room lighting technologies during the biological day, with different melanopsin excitations, such lighting was not sufficient to differentially protect against the effects of a 200 lux evening exposure of light on subjective or objective measures of alertness (Lok et al. 2022). These studies underscore the important interactions between the human biological clock and light's spectral properties, intensities, and timings, and that different output pathways may have different sensitivities. Subtle or even non-perceptible alterations to our lighting environment may have the ability to alter mind and behaviour, but they require both careful formulation and deployment.

11 Harnessing Light in the Built Environment

Light's role in the built environment is to support human outcomes – a simple concept that is devilishly complicated in practice. Complexity arises because people have such a wide range of visual, biological, and behavioural responses to light (Vetter et al. 2021, Ricketts et al. 2022). Focusing on only one or a few light-related outcomes always comes at the sacrifice of some other light-related outcome. For example, increasing interior light levels during daytime hours to support circadian health will increase the likelihood of visual discomfort and require more energy use. As another example, light source spectrum can be adjusted to support circadian health but doing so can perturb a light source's ability to render colours, distorting the appearance of skin and objects. Effective design first requires an appreciation of the factors influenced by light, and second an understanding of their interrelationships and trade-offs so that desired outcomes can be identified, prioritized, and addressed through design (Houser and Esposito 2021). Figure 9 illustrates the ways with which light as a stimulus can affect broad categories of human responses. The coloured boxes show schematic subdivisions in two broad categories, representing image and non-image forming pathways.

Image-forming responses to light include visual performance, visual experience, and visual comfort. Visual performance refers to how well light enables an observer to see and process visual information and might include measures of objective visual function. Visual experience includes psychological responses evoked by light, including perceptions of contrast, colour appearance and quality plus the emotional response and impressions as varied as relaxation (or tension), spaciousness (or enclosure), and brightness (or gloominess). Visual comfort refers to the degree to which there is freedom from glare, a condition of

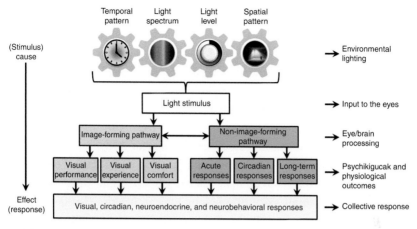

Figure 9 Schematic of the stimulus (top) response (bottom) relationship between light and human responses, emphasizing how environmental lighting variables influence visual, circadian, neuroendocrine, and neurobehavioural responses in humans. Reproduced from Houser and Esposito (2021).

vision that causes a reduction in the ability to see details caused by an unsuitable distribution or range of luminances.

Non-image-forming responses to light in applied settings can be considered by the time course of the response. Acute responses include pupil size, acute melatonin suppression, luminance adaptation, and short-term chromatic adaptation. The primary circadian response is circadian phase shift, important because it affects sleep and wake physiology and behaviours. Long-term responses influenced by light exposure may include stress, seasonal affective disorder, and depression. Because of the overlap in the spectral responses of the photopigments, and because there is crosstalk between neural pathways, any light source that is practical for architectural lighting will simultaneously elicit some degree of both image-forming and non-image-forming responses.

In applied settings such as residential, learning, and commercial environments, the human outcomes most commonly relevant to daily living are visual performance, visual experience, visual comfort, circadian phase-shifting, and alertness. The image-forming aspects of lighting have been subject to more than a century of research and are the basis for lighting industry recommended practices and design guidelines (e.g., DiLaura et al. 2011, Chartered Institution of Building Services Engineers 2018). It is only within the last few years that guidelines have begun to also promote non-image-forming aspects of light in applied settings (Deutsches Institut für

Normung 2013, Underwriters Laboratories Inc. 2019, International WELL Building Institute 2021, Brown et al. 2022). Though current health-related lighting guidelines vary in their specifics, they all consider the same set of variables: the timing and duration of light exposure, quantity of light that is a function of light level and spectrum, and the light exposure position. These factors are represented in the top row of Figure 9.

The temporal pattern of light exposure is the most important factor because the SCN, the master clock of the human body, keeps time by observing the natural world's diurnal pattern of light and dark. For people with conventional day (wake)/night (sleep) cycles, bright days and dark nights are an essential part of photobiological health. Health-oriented lighting design requires different lighting conditions at different times of day.

The next factor is light quantity, which is a function of both light level (intensity) and spectrum. Brighter light with proportionally more radiation near the peak of melanopsin spectral sensitivity will be more biologically potent than dim light with proportionally less light near the peak of melanopsin spectral sensitivity (Souman et al. 2018, Zele et al. 2018a, de Zeeuw et al. 2019, Brown 2020). The spectral composition of the light also affects colour rendering. Though there are several proposals for how to quantify the biological potency of light, the method with the most widespread international support is melanopic equivalent daylight illuminance (melanopic EDI, or mel-EDI for short), which was developed by the CIE (2018). Melanopic EDI is computed by weighing an absolute SPD by the melanopic action spectrum and equating the resulting quantity to a standardized model of daylight. It is expressed in units of lux.

All recommendations consider a vertical plane at seated height, which is intended to be a proxy for the position of an observer's eyes. Although there are statistical regularities that occur in lighting environments (Cohen 1964, Maloney 1986, Webler et al. 2019), in practice, gaze direction can substantially alter a person's light exposure. Looking at a bright window during daytime hours will produce a more biologically potent stimulus than looking towards a dimly lit wall.

Architects, lighting professionals, lighting equipment manufacturers, medical professionals, neuroscientists, building owners, and individuals all have a stake in determining practical design guidance to create healthy buildings and healthy lighting. The aforementioned guidelines are yet to undergo a full consensus-based process as would be required for ANSI (American National

Standards Institute), ISO (International Organization for Standardization), or IEC (International Electrotechnical Commission), but they nevertheless attempt to offer guidance that is consistent with known science. Understanding of the non-image-forming pathways continues to evolve, and it is useful to keep application advice simple even when the underlying science is complex. Looking to nature as inspiration is a good starting point, with bright days and dark nights (Wright et al. 2013) and with lighting linked to non-image-forming physiology, through specifying the ratio of melanopic to photopic excitation. Architecture driven by daylight design principles will support biological outcomes, and designs that are truly focused on human outcomes will also balance the needs for visibility, visual amenity, and visual comfort. Light in the visual environment presents a delightfully complex matrix of trade-offs and opportunities for supporting human outcomes.

12 Future Directions, Unknowns, and Conclusions

A comprehensive understanding of the non-image-forming pathways gives rise to an exciting field of so called 'photoceuticals', where light stimuli or lighting environments can be crafted in ways that specifically target non-image-forming physiology (Feigl et al. 2022). Just as for pharmaceuticals, careful consideration needs to be given to the dose (intensity), formulation (spectrum), and timing to maximize therapeutic effects while minimizing discomfort or side effects (Lucas et al. 2014). Image-forming and non-image-forming requirements of the light environment may not always be compatible, nevertheless there may be opportunities for overlap where lighting can maintain good image-forming properties (such as colour rendering) while the non-image-forming modulations remain imperceptible. Such lighting might dynamically promote alertness during the day and relaxation during the evening, encouraging more regular and sleep-wake rhythms that better align the biological clock with societal pressures such as school or work start times, ultimately supporting health and well-being in the process. Such lighting might also be leveraged to pre-empt disturbances to the non-image-forming pathway, for example, overdriving the circadian system at precisely the right times to help you more quickly recover from jetlag. Indeed, there are already commercially available room and wearable lighting products that make such claims. While they are sometimes theoretically grounded, more empirical data are required before wide adoption.

The visual pathways that are mediated by melanopsin signalling are exquisitely complex, and this complexity is often overlooked when considering driving these pathways to support positive human behaviors. Fundamentally, we are only now beginning to map the heterogeneity in the ipRGCs that are the neural substrate for signals that set image-forming and non-image-forming perceptual responses. In the retina, there is an array of ipRGC subtypes that differ in morphology, interconnections, electrophysiological responses, and cortical projections. These ipRGC responses are mediated by signals that originate through melanopsin, rod, and cone pathways, but the interplay of these signals is only beginning to be understood. Complexity is further increased when one considers that the signals that reach higher-order brain centres that control diverse aspects of behaviour could weight photic information differently from one another and themselves form complex circuits with other brain regions that might gate their activity.

Aside from simply controlling light to differentially activate photoreceptor classes, non-image-forming manipulations may become more powerful when modulated both spatially and temporally, maximizing the pathway response. Advanced optical, spectral, and psychophysical methods will need to be designed to account for the various integration properties of the rod and cone photoreceptor classes and their opponencies. Such modulations are achievable with research-grade optical apparatus, whereas precision targeting of image-forming and non-image-forming physiology in real-world environments presents additional challenges that require new solutions.

An important consideration is that of individual differences in our timings between circadian aspects of physiology, our behavioural preferences, and societal constraints (e.g., school start times). These differences mean that the factors that can reinforce healthy behaviours at one time or unhealthy behaviours at another (i.e., lighting or circadian rhythm phase) mean that a 'one size fits all' approach will be less effective, and ideally lighting interventions should be personalized to the individual. Broadly, we know that very bright days with very dark nights are good, but mimicking that in the urbanized community has proven difficult (often due to our own decision-making). And how does that change for a person that works rotating shifts, provides care at unusual times, or travels frequently across time zones for work? A more nuanced understanding of the intricate interactions of physiology, behavioural preferences, and societal pressures might lead in the future to personalized, and, importantly, validated interventions that maximize health and well-being.

In this Element, we have evaluated the current state of knowledge of melanopsin-mediated image-forming and non-image-forming vision. We have discussed the discovery of the ipRGC pathways and the current state of knowledge with special reference to humans. Psychophysical methods reveal the significance of melanopsin interrelations with rod and cone visual functions, including unique perceptual contributions from melanopsin. The pupil response is discussed as an objective biomarker of melanopsin function with utility for monitoring disease. The importance of light sensation for the circadian rhythms that set sleep-wake performance is established, and emerging paradigms to bias activation to the various photoreceptor inputs are evaluated. The dominance of electric lighting has resulted in manipulations to alter human cognitive perform-ance, with mixed results that may be dwarfed by individual differences or confounded by our incomplete knowledge of non-image-forming circuits. Lastly, we discussed an integrated approach to built environment lighting that balances image-forming and non-image forming objectives through mimicry of the natural light-dark cycles under which we evolved.

We have integrated a range of perspectives from vision scientists, circadian scientists, lighting professionals, and healthcare providers. As the reader can appreciate, what at the outset looks like a relatively simple task (the daily tracking of the diurnal patterns in light exposure that have existed for millions of years) turns out to be extraordinarily complicated. This complication points to many subtleties of physiology, brain, and behaviour that are yet be dis-covered. It is our hope that leveraging this emerging knowledge will lead to lightscapes that support both physical health and mental health, particularly in vulnerable populations who might not simply be able to enjoy strong sunlight during the day and dark skies at night (the institutionalized, those in climates with long, dark winters and bright summers, or even astronauts voyaging to distant planets). It will lead to new methods to detect, monitor, and treat melanopsin dysfunction in people with ophthalmic, systemic, and neurodegen-erative disease. It is important to recognize that lighting that drives ipRGC physiology represents a relatively passive intervention that is inexpensive and readily scalable. The effects of ipRGC-based modulations of brain and behav-iour could be significant for improving productivity, health, and well-being when viewed at the population level. It seems then that the future is bright, no matter with which visual system it is viewed.

References

Adhikari, P., B. Feigl, and A. J. Zele (2016a). 'Rhodopsin and melanopsin contributions to the early redilation phase of the post-illumination pupil response (PIPR)'. PLOS ONE **11**(8): e0161175.

Adhikari, P., B. Feigl, and A. J. Zele (2019a). 'The flicker pupil light response (fPLR)'. Translational Vision Science & Technology **8**(5): 29.

Adhikari, P., C. A. Pearson, A. M. Anderson, A. J. Zele, and B. Feigl (2015a). 'Effect of age and refractive error on the melanopsin mediated post-illumination pupil response (PIPR)'. Scientific Reports **5**: 17610.

Adhikari, P., A. J. Zele, D. Cao, J. Kremers, and B. Feigl (2019b). 'The melanopsin-directed white noise electroretinogram (wnERG)'. Vision Research **164**: 83–93.

Adhikari, P., A. J. Zele, and B. Feigl (2015b). 'The post-illumination pupil response (PIPR)'. Investigative Ophthalmology & Visual Science **56**(6): 3838–49.

Adhikari, P., A. J. Zele, R. Thomas, and B. Feigl (2016b). 'Quadrant field pupillometry detects melanopsin dysfunction in glaucoma suspects and early glaucoma'. Scientific Reports **6**: 33373.

Aguilar, M., and W. Stiles (1954). 'Saturation of the rod mechanism of the retina at high levels of stimulation'. Journal of Modern Optics **1**(1): 59–65.

al Enezi, J., V. Revell, T. Brown et al. (2011). 'A "melanopic" spectral efficiency function predicts the sensitivity of melanopsin photoreceptors to polychromatic lights'. Journal of Biological Rhythms **26**(4): 314–23.

Alkozei, A., R. Smith, D. A. Pisner et al. (2016). 'Exposure to blue light increases subsequent functional activation of the prefrontal cortex during performance of a working memory task'. Sleep **39**(9): 1671–80.

Allen, A. E., E. M. Hazelhoff, F. P. Martial, C. Cajochen, and R. J. Lucas (2018). 'Exploiting metamerism to regulate the impact of a visual display on alertness and melatonin suppression independent of visual appearance'. Sleep **41**(8): 1–15.

Allen, A. E., F. Martial, and R. Lucas (2019a). 'Applying the discovery of melanopsin photoreceptors in the human retina to enhancing the performance of visual displays'. Proceedings of SPIE 10942: Advances in Display Technologies IX **109420L**.

Allen, A. E., F. P. Martial, and R. J. Lucas (2019b). 'Form vision from melanopsin in humans'. Nature Communications **10**(1): 2274.

Allen, A. E., R. Storchi, F. P. Martial et al. (2014). 'Melanopsin-driven light adaptation in mouse vision'. Current Biology **24**(21): 2481–90.

Allen, A. E., R. Storchi, F. P. Martial, R. A. Bedford, and R. J. Lucas (2017). 'Melanopsin contributions to the representation of images in the early visual system'. Current Biology **27**(11): 1623–32.

Altimus, C. M., A. D. Güler, N. M. Alam et al. (2010). 'Rod photoreceptors drive circadian photoentrainment across a wide range of light intensities'. Nature Neuroscience **13**(9): 1107–12.

Anderson, R. S., M. B. Zlatkova, and S. Demirel (2002). 'What limits detection and resolution of short-wavelength sinusoidal gratings across the retina?' Vision Research **42**(8): 981–90.

Aston-Jones, G. (2005). 'Brain structures and receptors involved in alertness'. Sleep Medicine **6**: S3–S7.

Badia, P., B. Myers, M. Boecker, J. Culpepper, and J. R. Harsh (1991). 'Bright light effects on body temperature, alertness, EEG and behavior'. Physiology & Behavior **50**(3): 583–8.

Bailes, H. J., and R. J. Lucas (2013). 'Human melanopsin forms a pigment maximally sensitive to blue light (λmax $\approx$ 479 nm) supporting activation of Gq/11 and Gi/o signalling cascades'. Proceedings of the Royal Society B: Biological Sciences **280**(1759): 20122987.

Baraas, R. C., and A. J. Zele (2016). 'Psychophysical correlates of retinal processing'. Human Color Vision. J. Kremers, R. C. Baraas, and N. J. Marshall (eds.), Springer, Cham: 133–58.

Barbur, J. L., A. J. Harlow, and A. Sahraie (1992). 'Pupillary responses to stimulus structure, colour and movement'. Ophthalmic and Physiological Optics **12**(2): 137–41.

Barbur, J. L., A. Sahraie, A. Simmons, L. Weiskrantz, and S. C. R. Williams (1998). 'Residual processing of chromatic signals in the absence of a geniculostriate projection'. Vision Research **38**(21): 3447–53.

Barlow, H. B., and R. T. Verrillo (1976). 'Brightness sensation in a Ganzfeld'. Vision Research **16**(11): 1291–7.

Barnard, A. R., S. Hattar, M. W. Hankins, and R. J. Lucas (2006). 'Melanopsin regulates visual processing in the mouse retina'. Current Biology **16**(4): 389–95.

Barrionuevo, P. A., and D. Cao (2014). 'Contributions of rhodopsin, cone opsins, and melanopsin to postreceptoral pathways inferred from natural image statistics'. Journal of the Optical Society of America A **31**(4): A131–9.

Barrionuevo, P. A., and D. Cao (2016). 'Luminance and chromatic signals interact differently with melanopsin activation to control the pupil light response'. Journal of Vision **16**(11): 29.

Barrionuevo, P. A., J. J. McAnany, A. J. Zele, and D. Cao (2018). 'Non-linearities in the rod and cone photoreceptor inputs to the afferent pupil light response'. Frontiers in Neurology **9**: 1140.

Barrionuevo, P. A., N. Nicandro, J. J. McAnany et al. (2014). 'Assessing rod, cone and melanopsin contributions to human pupil flicker responses'. Investigative Ophthalmology & Visual Science **55**(2): 719–27.

Barrionuevo, P. A., C. Paz Filgueira, and D. Cao (2022). 'Is melanopsin activation affecting large field color-matching functions?" Journal of the Optical Society of America A **39**(6): 1104–10.

Baver, S. B., G. E. Pickard, P. J. Sollars, and G. E. Pickard (2008). 'Two types of melanopsin retinal ganglion cell differentially innervate the hypothalamic suprachiasmatic nucleus and the olivary pretectal nucleus'. European Journal of Neuroscience **27**(7): 1763–70.

Bellingham, J., S. S. Chaurasia, Z. Melyan et al. (2006). 'Evolution of mela-nopsin photoreceptors: discovery and characterization of a new melanopsin in nonmammalian vertebrates'. PLOS Biology **4**(8): e254.

Berson, D. M., F. A. Dunn, and M. Takao (2002). 'Phototransduction by retinal ganglion cells that set the circadian clock'. Science **295**(5557): 1070–3.

Besenecker, U. C., and J. D. Bullough (2016). 'Investigating visual mechanisms underlying scene brightness'. Lighting Research & Technology **49**(1): 16–32.

Borbély, A. A. (1982). 'A two process model of sleep regulation'. Human Neurobiology **1**(3): 195–204.

Borisuit, A., F. Linhart, J. L. Scartezzini, and M. Münch (2015). 'Effects of realistic office day lighting and electric lighting conditions on visual comfort, alertness and mood'. Lighting Research & Technology **47**(2): 192–209.

Brown, T. M. (2020). 'Melanopic illuminance defines the magnitude of human circadian light responses under a wide range of conditions'. Journal of Pineal Research **69**(1): e12655.

Brown, T. M., G. C. Brainard, C. Cajochen et al. (2022). 'Recommendations for daytime, evening, and nighttime indoor light exposure to best support physi-ology, sleep, and wakefulness in healthy adults'. PLOS Biology **20**(3): e3001571.

Brown, T. M., K. Thapan, J. Arendt, V. L. Revell, and D. J. Skene (2021). 'S-cone contribution to the acute melatonin suppression response in humans'. Journal of Pineal Research **71**(1): e12719.

Brown, T. M., S. Tsujimura, A. E. Allen et al. (2012). 'Melanopsin-based brightness discrimination in mice and humans'. Current Biology **22**(12): 1134–41.

Buck, S. (2003). 'Rod–cone interactions in human vision'. The Visual Neurosciences. L. M. Chalupa and J. S. Werner (eds.), MIT Press, Cambridge, MA., vol. 1: 863–79.

Bullough, J. D. (2018). 'Cone and melanopsin contributions to human brightness estimation: comment'. Journal of the Optical Society of America A **35** (10): 1780–2.

Cajochen, C. (2007). 'Alerting effects of light'. Sleep Medicine Reviews **11**(6): 453–64.

Cajochen, C., S. Frey, D. Anders et al. (2011). 'Evening exposure to a light-emitting diodes (LED)-backlit computer screen affects circadian physiology and cognitive performance'. Journal of Applied Physiology **110**(5): 1432–8.

Cajochen, C., J. M. Zeitzer, C. A. Czeisler, and D.-J. Dijk (2000). 'Dose-response relationship for light intensity and ocular and electroencephalographic correlates of human alertness'. Behavioural Brain Research **115**(1): 75–83.

Campbell, F. W., and D. G. Green (1965). 'Optical and retinal factors affecting visual resolution'. The Journal of Physiology **181**(3): 576–93.

Cao, D., A. Chang, and S. Gai (2018). 'Evidence for an impact of melanopsin activation on unique white perception'. Journal of the Optical Society of America A **35**(4): B287–91.

Cao, D., N. Nicandro, and P. A. Barrionuevo (2015). 'A five-primary photostimulator suitable for studying intrinsically photosensitive retinal ganglion cell functions in humans'. Journal of Vision **15**(1): 1–13.

Carle, C. F., A. C. James, M. Kolic, Y.-W. Loh, and T. Maddess (2011). 'High-resolution multifocal pupillographic objective perimetry in glaucoma'. Investigative Ophthalmology & Visual Science **52**(1): 604–10.

Chang, A.-M., N. Santhi, M. St Hilaire et al. (2012). 'Human responses to bright light of different durations'. The Journal of Physiology **590**(13): 3103–12.

Chang, A.-M., F. A. J. L. Scheer, and C. A. Czeisler (2011). 'The human circadian system adapts to prior photic history'. The Journal of Physiology **589**(5): 1095–102.

Chartered Institution of Building Services Engineers (2018). SLL Lighting Handbook. Chartered Institution of Building Service Engineers, London.

Chellappa, S. L. (2020). 'Individual differences in light sensitivity affect sleep and circadian rhythms'. Sleep **44**(2): zsaa214.

Chellappa, S. L., J. Q. M. Ly, C. Meyer et al. (2014). 'Photic memory for executive brain responses'. PNAS **111**(16): 6087–91.

Chellappa, S. L., R. Steiner, P. Blattner et al. (2011). 'Non-visual effects of light on melatonin, alertness and cognitive performance: can blue-enriched light keep us alert?'' PLOS ONE **6**(1): e16429.

Chellappa, S. L., R. Steiner, P. Oelhafen et al. (2013). 'Acute exposure to evening blue-enriched light impacts on human sleep'. Journal of Sleep Research **22**(5): 573–80.

Chen, C.-C., J. M. Foley, and D. H. Brainard (2000). 'Detection of chromoluminance patterns on chromoluminance pedestals I: threshold measurements'. Vision Research **40**(7): 773–88.

Chen, S.-K., T. C. Badea, and S. Hattar (2011). 'Photoentrainment and pupillary light reflex are mediated by distinct populations of ipRGCs'. Nature **476**(7358): 92–5.

Chougule, P. S., R. P. Najjar, M. T. Finkelstein, N. Kandiah, and D. Milea (2019). 'Light-induced pupillary responses in Alzheimer's disease'. Frontiers in Neurology **10**: 360.

Clarke, R. J., H. Zhang, and P. D. R. Gamlin (2003). 'Characteristics of the pupillary light reflex in the alert rhesus monkey'. Journal of Neurophysiology **89**(6): 3179–89.

Cohen, J. (1964). 'Dependency of the spectral reflectance curves of the Munsell color chips'. Psychonomic Science **1**(1): 369–70.

Collison, F. T., J. C. Park, G. A. Fishman, J. J. McAnany, and E. M. Stone (2015). 'Full-field pupillary light responses, luminance thresholds, and light discomfort thresholds in CEP290 Leber congenital amaurosis patients'. Investigative Ophthalmology & Visual Science **56**(12): 7130–6.

Commission Internationale de l'Éclairage (2018). CIE System for Metrology of Optical Radiation for ipRGC-Influenced Responses to Light CIE DIS 026/E:2018. Commission Internationale de l'Éclairage, Vienna.

Commission Internationale de l'Éclairage (2019). Position Statement on Non-Visual Effects of Light: Recommending Proper Light at the Proper Time. Commission Internationale de l'Éclairage, Vienna.

Crasson, M., and J. J. Legros (2005). 'Absence of daytime 50 Hz, 100 microT(rms) magnetic field or bright light exposure effect on human performance and psychophysiological parameters'. Bioelectromagnetics **26**(3): 225–33.

Crawford, B. H. (1936). 'The dependence of pupil size upon external light stimulus under static and variable conditions'. Proceedings of the Royal Society B: Biological Sciences **121**(823): 376–95.

Crook, J. D., C. M. Davenport, B. B. Peterson et al. (2009). 'Parallel ON and OFF cone bipolar inputs establish spatially coextensive receptive field structure of blue-yellow ganglion cells in primate retina'. The Journal of Neuroscience **29**(26): 8372–87.

Czeisler, C. A., J. F. Duffy, T. L. Shanahan et al. (1999). 'Stability, precision, and near-24-hour period of the human circadian pacemaker'. Science **284**(5423): 2177–81.

Dacey, D. M., H.-W. Liao, B. B. Peterson et al. (2005). 'Melanopsin-expressing ganglion cells in primate retina signal colour and irradiance and project to the LGN'. Nature **433**: 749–54.

Daguet, I., D. Bouhassira, and C. Gronfier (2019). 'Baseline pupil diameter is not a reliable biomarker of subjective sleepiness'. Frontiers in Neurology **10**: 108.

Dai, J., J. van der Vliet, D. F. Swaab, and R. M. Buijs (1998). 'Human retinohypothalamic tract as revealed by in vitro postmortem tracing'. Journal of Comparative Neurology **397**(3): 357–70.

Daneault, V., M. Hebert, G. Albouy et al. (2014). 'Aging reduces the stimulating effect of blue light on cognitive brain functions'. Sleep **37**(1): 85–96.

Daurat, A., J. Foret, O. Benoit, and G. Mauco (2000). 'Bright light during nighttime: effects on the circadian regulation of alertness and performance'. Biological Signals and Receptors **9**(6): 309–18.

Davies, W. I., T. K. Tamai, L. Zheng et al. (2015). 'An extended family of novel vertebrate photopigments is widely expressed and displays a diversity of function'. Genome Research **25**(11): 1666–79.

Davies, W. I., L. Zheng, S. Hughes et al. (2011). 'Functional diversity of melanopsins and their global expression in the teleost retina'. Cellular and Molecular Life Sciences **68**(24): 4115–32.

de Lange, H. (1954). 'Relationship between critical flicker-frequency and a set of low-frequency characteristics of the eye'. Journal of the Optical Society of America **44**(5): 380–8.

de Zeeuw, J., A. Papakonstantinou, C. Nowozin et al. (2019). 'Living in biological darkness: objective sleepiness and the pupillary light responses are affected by different metameric lighting conditions during daytime'. Journal of Biological Rhythms **34**(4): 410–31.

Deguchi, T. (1981). 'Rhodopsin-like photosensitivity of isolated chicken pineal gland'. Nature **290**: 706–7.

DeLawyer, T., S. Tsujimura, and K. Shinomori (2020). 'Relative contributions of melanopsin to brightness discrimination when hue and luminance also vary'. Journal of the Optical Society of America A **37**(4): A81–8.

DeMarco, P., J. Pokorny, and V. C. Smith (1992). 'Full-spectrum cone sensitivity functions for X-chromosome-linked anomalous trichromats'. Journal of the Optical Society of America A **9**(9): 1465–76.

Deutsches Institut für Normung (2013). DIN SPEC 67600:2013-04: biologically effective illumination – design guidelines. Deutsches Institut für Normung, Berlin.

Dey, A., A. J. Zele, B. Feigl, and P. Adhikari (2021). 'Threshold vision under full-field stimulation: revisiting the minimum number of quanta necessary to evoke a visual sensation'. Vision Research **180**: 1–10.

Dijk, D.-J., and C. A. Czeisler (1994). 'Paradoxical timing of the circadian rhythm of sleep propensity serves to consolidate sleep and wakefulness in humans'. Neuroscience Letters **166**(1): 63–8,

Dilaura, D. L., Houser, K. W., Mistrick, R. G., Steffy, G. R (2011). The Lighting Handbook 10th Edition: Reference and Application. Illuminating Engineering Society, New York.

Do, M. T. H., S. H. Kang, T. Xue et al. (2009). 'Photon capture and signalling by melanopsin retinal ganglion cells'. Nature **457**(7227): 281–7.

Dollins, A. B., H. J. Lynch, R. J. Wurtman, M. H. Deng, and H. R. Lieberman (1993). 'Effects of illumination on human nocturnal serum melatonin levels and performance'. Physiology & Behavior **53**(1): 153–60.

Dumpala, S., A. J. Zele, and B. Feigl (2019). 'Outer retinal structure and function deficits contribute to circadian disruption in patients with type 2 diabetes'. Investigative Ophthalmology & Visual Science **60**(6): 1870–8.

Eberhardt, L. V., G. Grön, M. Ulrich, A. Huckauf, and C. Strauch (2021). 'Direct voluntary control of pupil constriction and dilation: exploratory evidence from pupillometry, optometry, skin conductance, perception, and functional MRI'. International Journal of Psychophysiology **168**: 33–42.

Ecker, J. L., O. N. Dumitrescu, K. Y. Wong et al. (2010). 'Melanopsin-expressing retinal ganglion-cell photoreceptors: cellular diversity and role in pattern vision'. Neuron **67**(1): 49–60.

Emanuel, A. J., and M. T. H. Do (2015). 'Melanopsin tristability for sustained and broadband phototransduction'. Neuron **85**(5): 1043–55.

Esquiva, G., P. Lax, J. J. Pérez-Santonja, J. M. García-Fernández, and N. Cuenca (2017). 'Loss of melanopsin-expressing ganglion cell subtypes and dendritic degeneration in the aging human retina'. Frontiers in Aging Neuroscience **9**: 79.

Estevez, M. E., P. M. Fogerson, M. C. Ilardi et al. (2012). 'Form and function of the M4 cell, an intrinsically photosensitive retinal ganglion cell type contributing to geniculocortical vision'. The Journal of Neuroscience **32**(39): 13608–20.

Estevez, O., and H. Spekreijse (1982). 'The "silent substitution" method in visual research'. Vision Research **22**(6): 681–91.

Feigl, B., D.D. Carter, and A.J. Zele (2022). Photoreceptor enhanced light therapy (PELT): A framework for implementing biologically directed integrative lighting, LEUKOS: 1–14.

Feigl, B., D. Mattes, R. Thomas, and A. J. Zele (2011a). 'Intrinsically photosensitive (melanopsin) retinal ganglion cell function in glaucoma'. Investigative Ophthalmology & Visual Science **52**(7): 4362–7.

Feigl, B., G. Ojha, L. Hides, and A. J. Zele (2018). 'Melanopsin-driven pupil response and light exposure in non-seasonal major depressive disorder'. Frontiers in Neurology **9**: 764.

Feigl, B., and A. J. Zele (2014). 'Melanopsin-expressing intrinsically photosensitive retinal ganglion cells in retinal disease'. Optometry and Vision Science **91**(8): 894–903.

Feigl, B., A. J. Zele, S. M. Fader et al. (2011b). 'The post-illumination pupil response of melanopsin-expressing intrinsically photosensitive retinal ganglion cells in diabetes'. Acta Ophthalmologica **90**(3): e230–4.

Fernandez, D. C., Y.-T. Chang, S. Hattar, and S.-K. Chen (2016). 'Architecture of retinal projections to the central circadian pacemaker'. PNAS **113**(21): 6047–52.

Fernandez, D. C., P. M. Fogerson, L. Lazzerini Ospri et al. (2018). 'Light affects mood and learning through distinct retina-brain pathways'. Cell **175**(1): 71–84.e18.

Figueiro, M. G., A. Bierman, B. Plitnick, and M. S. Rea (2009). 'Preliminary evidence that both blue and red light can induce alertness at night'. BMC Neuroscience **10**: 105.

Foster, R. G., I. Provencio, D. Hudson et al. (1991). 'Circadian photoreception in the retinally degenerate mouse (rd/rd)'. Journal of Comparative Physiology A **169**(1): 39–50.

Freedman, M. S., R. J. Lucas, B. Soni et al. (1999). 'Regulation of mammalian circadian behavior by non-rod, non-cone, ocular photoreceptors'. Science **284**(5413): 502–4.

Gamlin, P. D. (2003). 'Pupils'. Encyclopedia of the Neurological Sciences. R. B. Daroff and M. J. Aminoff (eds.), Elsevier Science, Burlington, MA: 92–3.

Gamlin, P. D. R., D. H. McDougal, J. Pokorny et al. (2007). 'Human and macaque pupil responses driven by melanopsin-containing retinal ganglion cells'. Vision Research **47**(7): 946–54.

Gamlin, P. D. R., and A. Reiner (1991). 'The Edinger–Westphal nucleus: sources of input influencing accommodation, pupilloconstriction, and choroidal blood flow'. Journal of Comparative Neurology **306**(3): 425–38.

Gamlin, P. D. R., H. Zhang, A. Harlow, and J. L. Barbur (1998). 'Pupil responses to stimulus color, structure and light flux increments in the rhesus monkey'. Vision Research **38**(21): 3353–8.

Gislén, A., M. Dacke, R. H. H. Kröger et al. (2003). 'Superior underwater vision in a human population of sea gypsies'. Current Biology **13**(10): 833–6.

Gnyawali, S., B. Feigl, P. Adhikari, and A. J. Zele (2022). 'The role of melanopsin photoreception on visual attention linked pupil responses'. European Journal of Neuroscience **55**(8): 1986–2002.

Gooley, J. J., I. Ho Mien, M. A. St Hilaire et al. (2012). 'Melanopsin and rod–cone photoreceptors play different roles in mediating pupillary light responses during exposure to continuous light in humans'. The Journal of Neuroscience **32**(41): 14242–53.

Groos, G. A., and D. van der Kooy (1981). 'Functional absence of brain photoreceptors mediating entrainment of circadian rhythms in the adult rat'. Experientia **37**(1): 71–2.

Grünert, U., P. R. Jusuf, S. C. S. Lee, and D. T. Nguyen (2011). 'Bipolar input to melanopsin containing ganglion cells in primate retina'. Visual Neuroscience **28**(1): 39–50.

Grünert, U., and P. R. Martin (2021). 'Morphology, molecular characterization, and connections of ganglion cells in primate retina'. Annual Review of Vision Science **7**(1): 73–103.

Guler, A. D., J. L. Ecker, G. S. Lall et al. (2008). 'Melanopsin cells are the principal conduits for rod–cone input to non-image-forming vision'. Nature **453**(7191): 102–5.

Hankins, M. W., and R. J. Lucas (2002). 'The primary visual pathway in humans is regulated according to long-term light exposure through the action of a nonclassical photopigment'. Current Biology **12**(3): 191–8.

Hannibal, J., A. T. Christiansen, S. Heegaard, J. Fahrenkrug, and J. F. Kiilgaard (2017). 'Melanopsin expressing human retinal ganglion cells: subtypes, distribution, and intraretinal connectivity'. Journal of Comparative Neurology **525**(8): 1934–61.

Hannibal, J., L. Kankipati, C. E. Strang et al. (2014). 'Central projections of intrinsically photosensitive retinal ganglion cells in the macaque monkey'. Journal of Comparative Neurology **522**(10): 2231–48.

Hathibelagal, A. R., B. Feigl, J. Kremers, and A. J. Zele (2016). 'Correlated and uncorrelated invisible temporal white noise alters mesopic rod signaling'. Journal of the Optical Society of America A **33**(3): A93–103.

Hattar, S., M. Kumar, A. Park et al. (2006). 'Central projections of melanopsin-expressing retinal ganglion cells in the mouse'. Journal of Comparative Neurology **497**: 326–49.

Hattar, S., H.-W. Liao, M. Takao, D. M. Berson, and K.-W. Yau (2002). 'Melanopsin-containing retinal ganglion cells: architecture, projections, and intrinsic photosensitivity'. Science **295**(5557): 1065–70.

Hattar, S., R. J. Lucas, N. Mrosovsky et al. (2003). 'Melanopsin and rod–cone photoreceptive systems account for all major accessory visual functions in mice'. Nature **424**: 75–81.

Hecht, S., S. Shlaer, and M. H. Pirenne (1942). 'Energy, quanta, and vision'. Journal of General Physiology **25**(6): 819–40.

Hess, R. F., L. T. Sharpe, and K. Nordby (eds.). (1990). Night Vision: Basic, Clinical and Applied Aspects. Cambridge University Press, Cambridge.

Hexley, A. C., A. Özgür Yöntem, M. Spitschan, H. E. Smithson, and R. Mantiuk (2020). 'Demonstrating a multi-primary high dynamic range display system for vision experiments'. Journal of the Optical Society of America A **37**(4): A271–84.

Higuchi, S., A. Hida, S. Tsujimura et al. (2013). 'Melanopsin gene polymorphism I394T is associated with pupillary light responses in a dose-dependent manner'. PLOS ONE **8**(3): e60310.

Hood, D. C. (1998). 'Lower-level visual processing and models of light adaptation'. Annual Review of Psychology **49**(1): 503–35.

Horiguchi, H., J. Winawer, R. F. Dougherty, and B. A. Wandell (2013). 'Human trichromacy revisited'. PNAS **110**(3): E260–9.

Houser, K. W., P. R. Boyce, J. M. Zeitzer, and M. Herf (2020). 'Human-centric lighting: myth, magic or metaphor?' Lighting Research & Technology **53**(2): 97–118.

Houser, K. W., and T. Esposito (2021). 'Human-centric lighting: foundational considerations and a five-step design process'. Frontiers in Neurology **12**: 25.

Howarth, P. A., I. L. Bailey, S. M. Berman, G. Heron, and D. S. Greenhouse (1991). 'Location of nonlinear processes within the pupillarypathway'. Applied Optics **30**(16): 2100–5.

Hu, C., D. D. Hill, and K. Y. Wong (2013). 'Intrinsic physiological properties of the five types of mouse ganglion-cell photoreceptors'. Journal of Neurophysiology **109**(7): 1876–89.

Hughes, S., A. Jagannath, M. W. Hankins, R. G. Foster, and S. N. Peirson (2015). 'Photic regulation of clock systems'. Methods in Enzymology **552**: 125–43.

Hughes, S., A. Jagannath, J. Rodgers et al. (2016). 'Signalling by melanopsin (OPN4) expressing photosensitive retinal ganglion cells'. Eye **30**: 247–54.

Huiberts, L. M., K. C. Smolders, and Y. A. de Kort (2015). 'Shining light on memory: effects of bright light on working memory performance'. Behavioural Brain Research **294**: 234–45.

International WELL Building Institute (2021). Feature L03: Circadian Lighting Design. WELL Building Standard v2 Pilot Q2 2021 version.

International WELL Building Institute. https://v2.wellcertified.com/en/v/light/feature/3.

Iskra-Golec, I., I. Marek, A. Faliowicz, A. Zieba, and B. Honory (2000). 'Effects of bright light on performance and mood in morning and evening people'. Shiftwork in the 21st Century: Challenges for Research and Practice. S. Hornberger (ed.), Peter Lang, Wiesensteig; Frankfurt am Main; New York: 131–5.

Jacobs, G. H., M. Neitz, J. F. Deegan, and J. Neitz (1996). 'Trichromatic colour vision in New World monkeys'. Nature **382**(6587): 156–8.

Jagannath, A., S. Hughes, A. Abdelgany et al. (2015). 'Isoforms of melanopsin mediate different behavioral responses to light'. Current Biology **25**(18): 2430–4.

Jewett, M. E., R. E. Kronauer, and C. A. Czeisler (1994). 'Phase-amplitude resetting of the human circadian pacemaker via bright light: a further analysis'. Journal of Biological Rhythms **9**(3–4): 295–314.

Johnson, C. H. (1990). An Atlas of Phase Response Curves for Circadian and Circatidal Rhythms. Department of Biology, Vanderbilt University, Nashville, TN.

Johnson, R. F., R. Y. Moore, and L. P. Morin (1998). 'Loss of entrainment and anatomical plasticity after lesions of the hamster retinohypothalamic tract'. Brain Research **460**(2): 293–313.

Joo, H. R., B. B. Peterson, D. M. Dacey, S. Hattar, and S.-K. Chen (2013). 'Recurrent axon collaterals of intrinsically photosensitive retinal ganglion cells'. Visual Neuroscience **30**(4): 175–82.

Joyce, D. S., B. Feigl, D. Cao, and A. J. Zele (2015). 'Temporal characteristics of melanopsin inputs to the human pupil light reflex'. Vision Research **107**: 58–66.

Joyce, D. S., B. Feigl, G. Kerr, L. Roeder, and A. J. Zele (2018). 'Melanopsin-mediated pupil function is impaired in Parkinson's disease'. Scientific Reports **8**(7796): 1–9.

Joyce, D. S., B. Feigl, and A. J. Zele (2016a). 'The effects of short-term light adaptation on the human post-illumination pupil response'. Investigative Ophthalmology & Visual Science **57**(13): 5672–80.

Joyce, D. S., B. Feigl, and A. J. Zele (2016b). 'Melanopsin-mediated post-illumination pupil response in the peripheral retina'. Journal of Vision **16**(8): 1–15.

Jusuf, P. R., S. C. Lee, J. Hannibal, and U. Grunert (2007). 'Characterization and synaptic connectivity of melanopsin-containing ganglion cells in the primate retina'. European Journal of Neuroscience **26**(10): 2906–21.

Kankipati, L., C. A. Girkin, and P. D. Gamlin (2011). 'The post-illumination pupil response is reduced in glaucoma patients'. Investigative Ophthalmology & Visual Science **52**(5): 2287–92.

Kardon, R., S. C. Anderson, T. G. Damarjian et al. (2009). 'Chromatic pupil responses: preferential activation of the melanopsin-mediated versus outer photoreceptor-mediated pupil light reflex'. Ophthalmology **116**(8): 1564–73.

Kawasaki, A., K. Herbst, B. Sander, and D. Milea (2010). 'Selective wavelength pupillometry in Leber hereditary optic neuropathy'. Clinical & Experimental Ophthalmology **38**(3): 322–4.

Kawasaki, A., and R. H. Kardon (2007). 'Intrinsically photosensitive retinal ganglion cells'. Journal of Neuro-Ophthalmology **27**(3): 195–204.

Keeler, C. E. (1927). 'Iris movements in blind mice'. American Journal of Physiology **81**(1): 107–12.

Keeler, C. E., E. Sutcliffe, and E. L. Chaffee (1928). 'Normal and "rodless" retinae of the house mouse with respect to the electromotive force generated through stimulation by light'. PNAS **14**(6): 477–84.

Kelbsch, C., J. Lange, H. Wilhelm et al. (2020). 'Chromatic pupil campimetry reveals functional defects in exudative age-related macular degeneration with differences related to disease activity'. Translational Vision Science & Technology **9**(6): 5.

Kelbsch, C., T. Strasser, Y. Chen et al. (2019). 'Standards in pupillography'. Frontiers in Neurology **10**: 129.

Kelly, D. H. (1961). 'Flicker fusion and harmonic analysis'. Journal of the Optical Society of America **51**(8): 917–18.

Khalsa, S. B. S., M. E. Jewett, C. Cajochen, and C. A. Czeisler (2003). 'A phase-response curve to single bright light pulses in human subjects'. Journal of Physiology **549**(pt. 3): 945–52.

König, A., and C. Dieterici (1893). 'Die Grünempfindungen in normalen und anomalen Farbensystemen und ihre Intensitäts-Verteilung im Spektrum'.Zeitschrift für Psychologie und Physiologie der Sinnesorgane **4**: 241–347.

Kuffler, S. W. (1953). 'Discharge patterns and functional organization of mammalian retina'. Journal of Neurophysiology **16**(1): 37–68.

La Morgia, C., V. Carelli, and M. Carbonelli (2018). 'Melanopsin retinal ganglion cells and pupil: clinical implications for neuro-ophthalmology'. Frontiers in Neurology **9**: 1047.

Lall, G. S., V. L. Revell, H. Momiji et al. (2010). 'Distinct contributions of rod, cone, and melanopsin photoreceptors to encoding irradiance'. Neuron **66**(3): 417–28.

Laurenzo, S. A., R. Kardon, J. Ledolter et al. (2016). 'Pupillary response abnormalities in depressive disorders'. Psychiatry Research **246**: 492–9.

Lavoie, S., J. Paquet, B. Selmaoui, M. Rufiange, and M. Dumont (2003) 'Vigilance levels during and after bright light exposure in the first half of the night'. Chronobiology International **20**(6): 1019–38.

Lee, B. B., V. C. Smith, J. Pokorny, and J. Kremers (1997). 'Rod inputs to macaque ganglion cells'. Vision Research **37**(20): 2813–28.

Lee, S.-i., A. Hida, S. Tsujimura et al. (2013). 'Association between melanopsin gene polymorphism (I394 T) and pupillary light reflex is dependent on light wavelength'. Journal of Physiological Anthropology **32**(1): 16.

Lee, S. C. S., P. R. Jusuf, and U. Grünert (2004). 'S-cone connections of the diffuse bipolar cell type DB6 in macaque monkey retina'. Journal of Comparative Neurology **474**(3): 353–63.

Lee, S. I., A. Hida, S. Kitamura, K. Mishima, and S. Higuchi (2014). 'Association between the melanopsin gene polymorphism OPN4*Ile 394Thr and sleep/wake timing in Japanese university students'. Journal of Physiological Anthropology **33**: 9.

LeGates, T. A., D. C. Fernandez, and S. Hattar (2014). 'Light as a central modulator of circadian rhythms, sleep and affect'. Nature Reviews: Neuroscience **15**: 443.

Lennie, P., J. Pokorny, and V. C. Smith (1993). 'Luminance'. Journal of the Optical Society of America A **10**(6): 1283–93.

Leproult, R., O. van Reeth, M. M. Byrne, J. Sturis, and E. Van Cauter (1997). 'Sleepiness, performance, and neuroendocrine function during sleep deprivation: effects of exposure to bright light or exercise'. Journal of Biological Rhythms **12**(3): 245–58.

Liao, H.-W., X. Ren, B. B. Peterson et al. (2016). 'Melanopsin-expressing ganglion cells on macaque and human retinas form two morphologically distinct populations'. Journal of Comparative Neurology **524**(14): 2845–72.

Lockley, S. W., E. E. Evans, F. A. Scheer et al. (2006). 'Short-wavelength sensitivity for the direct effects of light on alertness, vigilance, and the waking electroencephalogram in humans'. Sleep **29**(2): 161–8.

Lok, R., D. S. Joyce, and J. M. Zeitzer (2022). 'Impact of daytime spectral tuning on cognitive function'. Journal of Photochemistry and Photobiology B: Biology **230**: 112439.

Lowenstein, O., and I. E. Loewenfeld (1969). 'The Pupil'. The Eye. H. Davson (ed.), Academic Press, New York: 255–337.

Lucas, R. J., R. H. Douglas, and R. G. Foster (2001). 'Characterization of an ocular photopigment capable of driving pupillary constriction in mice'. Nature Neuroscience **4**(6): 621–6.

Lucas, R. J., S. Hattar, M. Takao et al. (2003). 'Diminished pupillary light reflex at high irradiances in melanopsin-knockout mice'. Science **299**(5604): 245–7.

Lucas, R. J., S. N. Peirson, D. M. Berson et al. (2014). 'Measuring and using light in the melanopsin age'. Trends in Neurosciences **37**(1): 1–9.

Lüdtke, H., B. Wilhelm, M. Adler, F. Schaeffel, and H. Wilhelm (1998). 'Mathematical procedures in data recording and processing of pupillary fatigue waves'. Vision Research **38**(19): 2889–96.

MacLeod, D. I. A. (1978). 'Visual sensitivity'. Annual Review of Psychology **29**(1): 613–45.

Makous, W. (2003). 'Scotopic vision'. The Visual Neurosciences. L. M. Chalupa and J. S. Werner (eds.), MIT Press, Cambridge, MA, vol. 1: 838–50.

Maloney, L. T. (1986). 'Evaluation of linear models of surface spectral reflectance with small numbers of parameters'. Journal of the Optical Society of America A **3**(10): 1673–83.

Mansfield, R. J. W. (1976). 'Visual adaptation: retinal transduction, brightness and sensitivity'. Vision Research **16**(7): 679–90.

Markwell, E. L., B. Feigl, and A. J. Zele (2010). 'Intrinsically photosensitive melanopsin retinal ganglion cell contributions to the pupillary light reflex and circadian rhythm'. Clinical and Experimental Optometry **93**(3): 137–49.

Masri, R. A., K. A. Percival, A. Koizumi, P. R. Martin, and U. Grunert (2019). 'Survey of retinal ganglion cell morphology in marmoset'. Journal of Comparative Neurology **527**(1): 236–58.

Maxwell, J. C. (1855). 'Experiments on colour, as perceived by the eye, with remarks on colour-blindness'. Transactions of the Royal Society of Edinburgh **21**: 275–98.

Maynard, M. L., A. J. Zele, and B. Feigl (2015). 'Melanopsin-mediated post-illumination pupil response in early age-related macular degeneration'. Investigative Ophthalmology & Visual Science **56**(11): 6906–13.

Maynard, M. L., A. J. Zele, A. S. Kwan, and B. Feigl (2017). 'Intrinsically photosensitive retinal ganglion cell function, sleep efficiency and depression in advanced age-related Macular Degeneration'. Investigative Ophthalmology & Visual Science **58**(2): 990–6.

McDougal, D. H., and P. D. Gamlin (2010). 'The influence of intrinsically-photosensitive retinal ganglion cells on the spectral sensitivity and response dynamics of the human pupillary light reflex'. Vision Research **50**(1): 72–87.

Metha, A. B., and P. Lennie (2001). 'Transmission of spatial information in S-cone pathways'. Visual Neuroscience **18**(6): 961–72.

Milner, E. S., and M. T. H. Do (2017). 'A population representation of absolute light intensity in the mammalian retina'. Cell **171**(4): 865–76.e816.

Milosavljevic, N., R. Storchi, C. G. Eleftheriou et al. (2018). 'Photoreceptive retinal ganglion cells control the information rate of the optic nerve'. PNAS **115**(50): E11817–26.

Mistlberger, R. E., and B. Rusak (2005). 'Circadian Rhythms in Mammals: Formal Properties and Environmental Influences'. Principles and Practice of Sleep Medicine. M. H. Kryger, T. Roth, and W. C. Dement (eds.), Elsevier, Philadelphia. 321–334.

Mollon, J. D., J. M. Bosten, D. H. Peterzell, and M. A. Webster (2017). 'Individual differences in visual science: what can be learned and what is good experimental practice?' Vision Research **141**: 4–15.

Moore, R. Y. (1995). 'Organization of the Mammalian Circadian System'. Circadian Clocks and Their Adjustment. John Wiley and Sons, Chichester. Ciba Foundation Symposium 183: 88–106.

Moore, R. Y., and N. J. Lenn (1972). 'A retinohypothalamic projection in the rat'. Journal of Comparative Neurology **146**(1): 1–9.

Moore, R. Y., J. C. Speh, and J. P. Card (1995). 'The retinohypothalamic tract originates from a distinct subset of retinal ganglion cells'. Journal of Comparative Neurology **352**: 351–66.

Moura, A. L. A., B. V. Nagy, C. La Morgia et al. (2013). 'The pupil light reflex in Leber's hereditary optic neuropathy: evidence for preservation of mela-nopsin-expressing retinal ganglion cells'. Investigative Ophthalmology & Visual Science **54**(7): 4471–7.

Münch, M., S. Kobialka, R. Steiner et al. (2006). 'Wavelength-dependent effects of evening light exposure on sleep architecture and sleep EEG power density in men'. American Journal of Physiology – Regulatory, Integrative and Comparative Physiology **290**(5): R1421–8.

Münch, M., L. Léon, S. V. Crippa, and A. Kawasaki (2012). 'Circadian and wake-dependent effects on the pupil light reflex in response to narrow-bandwidth light pulses'. Investigative Ophthalmology & Visual Science **53**(8): 4546–55.

Munteanu, T., K. J. Noronha, A. C. Leung et al. (2018). 'Light-dependent pathways for dopaminergic amacrine cell development and function'. eLife **7**: e39866.

Mure, L. S. (2021). 'Intrinsically photosensitive retinal ganglion cells of the human retina'. Frontiers in Neurology **12**: 636330.

Mure, L. S., F. Vinberg, A. Hanneken, and S. Panda (2019). 'Functional diversity of human intrinsically photosensitive retinal ganglion cells'. Science **366**(6470): 1251–5.

Murray, I. J., J. Kremers, D. McKeefry, and N. R. A. Parry (2018). 'Paradoxical pupil responses to isolated M-cone increments'. Journal of the Optical Society of America A **35**(4): B66–71.

Nagel, W. (1924). 'Adaptation, Twilight Vision and the Duplicity Theory'. Helmholtz's Treatise on Physiological Optics, translated from the third German edition. Optical Society of America, Rochester, NY, vol. 1.

Najjar, R. P., and J. M. Zeitzer (2016). 'Temporal integration of light flashes by the human circadian system'. Journal of Clinical Investigation **126**(3): 938–47.

Nasir-Ahmad, S., S. C. S. Lee, P. R. Martin, and U. Grünert (2017). 'Melanopsin-expressing ganglion cells in human retina: morphology, distribution, and synaptic connections'. Journal of Comparative Neurology **527**: 1–16.

Nathans, J., T. Piantanida, R. Eddy, T. Shows, and D. Hogness (1986). 'Molecular genetics of inherited variation in human color vision'. Science **232**(4747): 203–10.

Nelson, R. J., and I. Zucker (1981). 'Photoperiodic control of reproduction in olfactory-bulbectomized rats'. Neuroendocrinology **32**(5): 266–71.

Newkirk, G. S., M. Hoon, R. O. Wong, and P. B. Detwiler (2013). 'Inhibitory inputs tune the light response properties of dopaminergic amacrine cells in mouse retina'. Journal of Neurophysiology **110**(2): 536–52.

O'Brien, P. M., and P. J. O'Connor (2000). 'Effect of bright light on cycling performance'. Medicine & Science in Sports & Exercise **32**(2): 439–47.

Okamoto, Y., M. S. Rea, and M. G. Figueiro (2014). 'Temporal dynamics of EEG activity during short- and long-wavelength light exposures in the early morning'. BMC Research Notes **7**: 113.

Oken, B. S., M. C. Salinsky, and S. M. Elsas (2006). 'Vigilance, alertness, or sustained attention: physiological basis and measurement'. Clinical Neurophysiology **117**(9): 1885–901.

Ortuño-Lizarán, I., G. Esquiva, T. G. Beach et al. (2018). 'Degeneration of human photosensitive retinal ganglion cells may explain sleep and circadian rhythms disorders in Parkinson's disease'. Acta Neuropathologica Communications **6**(1): 90.

Ostrin, L. A. (2018). 'The ipRGC-driven pupil response with light exposure and refractive error in children'. Ophthalmic and Physiological Optics **38**(5): 503–15.

Ostrin, L. A., C. E. Strang, K. Chang et al. (2018). 'Immunotoxin-induced ablation of the intrinsically photosensitive retinal ganglion cells in rhesus monkeys'. Frontiers in Neurology **9**: 1000.

Panda, S., T. K. Sato, A. M. Castrucci et al. (2002). 'Melanopsin (Opn4) requirement for normal light-induced circadian phase shifting'. Science **298**(5601): 2213–16.

Pant, M., A. J. Zele, B. Feigl, and P. Adhikari (2021). 'Light adaptation characteristics of melanopsin'. Vision Research **188**: 126–38.

Park, J. C., Y.-F. Chen, N. P. Blair et al. (2017). 'Pupillary responses in non-proliferative diabetic retinopathy'. Scientific Reports **7**(1): 44987.

Park, J. C., and J. J. McAnany (2015). 'Effect of stimulus size and luminance on the rod-, cone-, and melanopsin-mediated pupillary light reflex'. Journal of Vision **15**(3): 1–13.

Park, J. C., A. L. Moura, A. S. Raza et al. (2011). 'Toward a clinical protocol for assessing rod, cone, and melanopsin contributions to the human pupil response'. Investigative Ophthalmology & Visual Science **52**(9): 6624–35.

Patterson, S. S., J. A. Kuchenbecker, J. R. Anderson, M. Neitz, and J. Neitz (2020). 'A color vision circuit for non-image-forming vision in the primate retina'. Current Biology **30**(7): 1269–74.e1262.

Peirson, S. N., S. Thompson, M. W. Hankins, and R. G. Foster (2005). 'Mammalian photoentrainment: results, methods, and approaches'. Methods in Enzymology **393**: 697–726.

Perrin, F., P. Peigneux, S. Fuchs et al. (2004). 'Nonvisual responses to light exposure in the human brain during the circadian night'. Current Biology **14**(20): 1842–6.

Phillips, A. J. K., P. Vidafar, A. C. Burns et al. (2019). 'High sensitivity and interindividual variability in the response of the human circadian system to evening light'. PNAS **116**(24): 12019–24.

Phipps-Nelson, J., J. R. Redman, D.-J. Dijk, and S. M. W. Rajaratnam (2003). 'Daytime exposure to bright light, as compared to dim light, decreases sleepiness and improves psychomotor vigilance performance'. Sleep **26**(6): 695–700.

Phipps-Nelson, J., J. R. Redman, L. J. Schlangen, and S. M. Rajaratnam (2009). 'Blue light exposure reduces objective measures of sleepiness during prolonged nighttime performance testing'. Chronobiology International **26**(5): 891–912.

Pickard, G. E. (1980). 'Morphological characteristics of retinal ganglion cells projecting to the suprachiasmatic nucleus: a horseradish peroxidase study'. Brain Research **183**(2): 458–65.

Pierson, R. J., and M. B. Carpenter (1974). 'Anatomical analysis of pupillary reflex pathways in the rhesus monkey'. Journal of Comparative Neurology **158**(2): 121–43.

Pires, S. S., S. Hughes, M. Turton et al. (2009). 'Differential expression of two distinct functional isoforms of melanopsin (Opn4) in the mammalian retina'. The Journal of Neuroscience **29**(39): 12332–42.

Pokorny, J., M. Lutze, D. Cao, and A. J. Zele (2006). 'The color of night: surface color perception under dim illuminations'. Visual Neuroscience **23**(3/4): 525–30.

Pokorny, J., H. Smithson, and J. Quinlan (2004). 'Photostimulator allowing independent control of rods and the three cone types'. Visual Neuroscience **21**(3): 263–7.

Pottackal, J., H. L. Walsh, P. Rahmani et al. (2021). 'Photoreceptive ganglion cells drive circuits for local inhibition in the mouse retina'. Journal of Neuroscience **41**(7): 1489–504.

Prigge, C. L., P. T. Yeh, N. F. Liou et al. (2016). 'M1 ipRGCs influence visual function through retrograde signaling in the retina'. Journal of Neuroscience **36**(27): 7184–97.

Provencio, I., H. M. Cooper, and R. G. Foster (1998a). 'Retinal projections in mice with inherited degeneration: implications for circadian photoentrainment'. Journal of Comparative Neurology **395**(4): 417–39.

Provencio, I., and R. G. Foster (1995). 'Circadian rhythms in mice can be regulated by photoreceptors with cone-like characteristics'. Brain Research **694**(1–2): 183–90.

Provencio, I., G. Jiang, W. J. de Grip, W. P. Hayes, and M. D. Rollag (1998b). 'Melanopsin: an opsin in melanophores, brain, and eye'. PNAS **95**(1): 340–5.

Provencio, I., I. R. Rodriguez, G. Jiang et al. (2000). 'A novel human opsin in the inner retina'. Journal of Neuroscience **20**(2): 600–5.

Provencio, I., M. D. Rollag, and A. M. Castrucci (2002). 'Photoreceptive net in the mammalian retina: this mesh of cells may explain how some blind mice can still tell day from night'. Nature **415**(6871): 493.

Purkyně, J. E. (1823). Beobachtungen und Versuche zur Physiologie der Sinne. In Commission der JG Calve'schen Buchhandlung, Prague.

Quattrochi, L. E., M. E. Stabio, I. Kim et al. (2019). 'The M6 cell: a small-field bistratified photosensitive retinal ganglion cell'. Journal of Comparative Neurology **527**(1): 297–311.

Rahman, S. A., E. E. Flynn-Evans, D. Aeschbach et al. (2014). 'Diurnal spectral sensitivity of the acute alerting effects of light'. Sleep **37**(2): 271–81.

Rahman, S. A., S. Marcu, C. M. Shapiro, T. J. Brown, and R. F. Casper (2011). 'Spectral modulation attenuates molecular, endocrine, and neurobehavioral disruption induced by nocturnal light exposure'. American Journal of Physiology: Endocrinology and Metabolism **300**(3): E518–27.

Rahman, S. A., C. M. Shapiro, F. Wang et al. (2013). 'Effects of filtering visual short wavelengths during nocturnal shiftwork on sleep and performance'. Chronobiology International **30**(8): 951–62.

Rahman, S. A., M. A. St Hilaire, A. M. Chang et al. (2017a). 'Circadian phase resetting by a single short-duration light exposure'. JCI Insight **2**(7): e89494.

Rahman, S. A., M. A. St Hilaire, and S. W. Lockley (2017b). 'The effects of spectral tuning of evening ambient light on melatonin suppression, alertness and sleep'. Physiology & Behavior **177**: 221–9.

Reeves, A. (2003). 'Visual Adaptation'. The Visual Neurosciences. L. M. Chalupa and J. S. Werner (eds.), MIT Press, Cambridge, MA, vol. 1: 851–62.

Reifler, A. N., A. P. Chervenak, M. E. Dolikian et al. (2015). 'All spiking, sustained ON displaced amacrine cells receive gap-junction input from melanopsin ganglion cells'. Current Biology **25**(21): 2763–73.

Ricketts, E., D. S. Joyce, A. J. Rissman et al. (2022). 'Electric lighting, adolescent sleep and circadian outcomes, and recommendations for improving light health'. Sleep Medicine Reviews **64**: 1–10.

Rimmer, D. W., D. B. Boivin, T. L. Shanahan et al. (2000). 'Dynamic resetting of the human circadian pacemaker by intermittent bright light'. American Journal of Physiology **279**: R1574–9.

Rodgers, J., S. Hughes, C. A. Pothecary et al. (2018a). 'Defining the impact of melanopsin missense polymorphisms using in vivo functional rescue'. Human Molecular Genetics **27**(15): 2589–603.

Rodgers, J., S. N. Peirson, S. Hughes, and M. W. Hankins (2018b). 'Functional characterisation of naturally occurring mutations in human melanopsin'. Cellular and Molecular Life Sciences **75**(19): 3609–24.

Roecklein, K., P. Wong, N. Ernecoff et al. (2013). 'The post illumination pupil response is reduced in seasonal affective disorder'. Psychiatry Research **210**(1): 150–8.

Roecklein, K. A., K. J. Rohan, W. C. Duncan et al. (2009). 'A missense variant (P10L) of the melanopsin (OPN4) gene in seasonal affective disorder'. Journal of Affective Disorders **114**(1–3): 279–85.

Roecklein, K. A., P. M. Wong, P. L. Franzen et al. (2012). 'Melanopsin gene variations interact with season to predict sleep onset and chronotype'. Chronobiology International **29**(8): 1036–47.

Roenneberg,T., and R. G. Foster (1997). 'Twilight times: light and the circadian system'. Photochemistry and Photobiology **66**(5): 549–61.

Ruby, N. F., T. J. Brennan, X. Xie et al. (2002). 'Role of melanopsin in circadian responses to light'. Science **298**(5601): 2211–13.

Rukmini, A. V., M. C. Chew, M. T. Finkelstein et al. (2019a). 'Effects of low and moderate refractive errors on chromatic pupillometry'. Scientific Reports **9**(1): 4945.

Rukmini, A. V., D. Milea, and J. J. Gooley (2019b). 'Chromatic pupillometry methods for assessing photoreceptor health in retinal and optic nerve diseases'. Frontiers in Neurology **10**: 76.

Rushton, W. A. H. (1972). 'Review lecture: pigments and signals in colour vision'. Journal of Physiology **220**(3): 1–31.

Sadun, A. A., J. D. Schaechter, and L. E. H. Smith (1984). 'A retinohypothalamic pathway in man: light mediation of circadian rhythms'. Brain Research **302**: 371–7.

Sahin, L., and M. G. Figueiro (2013). 'Alerting effects of short-wavelength (blue) and long-wavelength (red) lights in the afternoon'. Physiology & Behavior **116–17**: 1–7.

Sahin, L., B. M. Wood, B. Plitnick, and M. G. Figueiro (2014). 'Daytime light exposure: effects on biomarkers, measures of alertness, and performance'. Behavioural Brain Research **274**: 176–85.

Sand, A., T. M. Schmidt, and P. Kofuji (2012). 'Diverse types of ganglion cell photoreceptors in the mammalian retina'. Progress in Retinal and Eye Research **31**(4): 287–302.

Sanes, J. R., and R. H. Masland (2015). 'The types of retinal ganglion cells: current status and implications for neuronal classification'. Annual Review of Neuroscience **38**(1): 221–46.

Schmidt, T. M., N. M. Alam, S. Chen et al. (2014). 'A role for melanopsin in alpha retinal ganglion cells and contrast detection'. Neuron **82**(4): 781–8.

Schmidt, T. M., S. K. Chen, and S. Hattar (2011). 'Intrinsically photosensitive retinal ganglion cells: many subtypes, diverse functions'. Trents in Neurosciences **34**(11): 572–80.

Schmidt, T. M., and P. Kofuji (2009). 'Functional and morphological differences among intrinsically photosensitive retinal ganglion cells'. Journal of Neuroscience **29**(2): 476–82.

Schoonderwoerd, R. A., M. de Rover, J. A. M. Janse et al. (2022). 'The photobiology of the human circadian clock'. PNAS **119**(13): e2118803119.

Schrödinger,E. (1925). 'On the relation of the four colors to the three color theory'. Meeting reports. Department 2a, Mathematics, Astronomy, Physics, Meteorology and Mechanics, Academy of Sciences in Vienna, Mathematical and Natural Science Class **134**: 471.

Sekaran, S., R. G. Foster, R. J. Lucas, and M. W. Hankins (2003). 'Calcium imaging reveals a network of intrinsically light-sensitive inner-retinal neurons'. Current Biology **13**(15): 1290–8.

Sexton, T. J., M. Golczak, K. Palczewski, and R. N. van Gelder (2012). 'Melanopsin is highly resistant to light and chemical bleaching in vivo'. Journal of Biological Chemistry **287**(25): 20888–97.

Shapiro, A. G., J. Pokorny, and V. C. Smith (1996). 'Cone–rod receptor spaces with illustrations that use CRT phosphor and light-emitting-diode spectra'. Journal of the Optical Society of America A **13**(12): 2319–28.

Shapiro, C. M., C. Auch, M. Reimer et al. (2006). 'A new approach to the construct of alertness'. Journal of Psychosomatic Research **60**(6): 595–603.

Shapley, R., and C. Enroth-Cugell (1984). 'Visual adaptation and retinal gain controls'. Progress in Retinal Research **3**: 263–346.

Shevell, S. K., and F. A. A. Kingdom (2007). 'Color in complex scenes'. Annual Review of Psychology **59**(1): 143–66.

Smith, V. C., J. Pokorny, B. B. Lee, and D. M. Dacey (2008). 'Sequential processing in vision: the interaction of sensitivity regulation and temporal dynamics'. Vision Research **48**(26): 2649–56.

Smolders, K. C., and Y. A. de Kort (2014). 'Bright light and mental fatigue: effects on alertness, vitality, performance and physiological arousal'. Journal of Environmental Psychology **39**: 77–91.

Smolders, K. C., Y. A. de Kort, and P. J. Cluitmans (2012). 'A higher illuminance induces alertness even during office hours: findings on subjective measures, task performance and heart rate measures'. Physiology & Behavior **107**(1): 7–16.

Souman, J. L., T. Borra, I. de Goijer et al. (2018). 'Spectral tuning of white light allows for strong reduction in melatonin suppression without changing illumination level or color temperature'. Journal of Biological Rhythms **33**(4): 420–31.

Souman, J. L., A. M. Tinga, S. F. Te Pas, R. van Ee, and B. N. S. Vlaskamp (2017). 'Acute alerting effects of light: a systematic literature review'. Behavioural Brain Research **337**: 228–39.

Spitschan, M., G. K. Aguirre, and D. H. Brainard (2015). 'Selective stimulation of penumbral cones reveals perception in the shadow of retinal blood vessels'. PLOS ONE **10**(4): e0124328.

Spitschan, M., A. S. Bock, J. Ryan et al. (2017). 'The human visual cortex response to melanopsin-directed stimulation is accompanied by a distinct perceptual experience'. PNAS **114**(46): 12291–6.

Spitschan, M., S. Jain, D. H. Brainard, and G. K. Aguirre (2014). 'Opponent melanopsin and S-cone signals in the human pupillary light response'. PNAS **111**(43): 15568–72.

Spitschan, M., R. Lazar, E. Yetik, and C. Cajochen (2019). 'No evidence for an S cone contribution to acute neuroendocrine and alerting responses to light'. Current Biology **29**(24): R1297–8.

St Hilaire, M. A., J. J. Gooley, S. B. S. Khalsa et al. (2012). 'Human phase response curve to a 1 h pulse of bright white light'. Journal of Physiology **590**(13): 3035–45.

Stabell, B., and U. Stabell (2009). Duplicity Theory of Vision: From Newton to the Present. Cambridge University Press, Cambridge.

Stabio, M. E., S. Sabbah, L. E. Quattrochi et al. (2018). 'The M5 cell: a color-opponent intrinsically photosensitive retinal ganglion cell'. Neuron **97**(1): 251.

Stanley, P. A., and A. K. Davies (1995). 'The effect of field of view size on steady-state pupil diameter'. Ophthalmic and Physiological Optics **15**(6): 601–3.

Stark, L., and P. M. Sherman (1957). 'A servoanalytic study of consensual pupil reflex to light'. Journal of Neurophysiology **20**(1): 17–26.

Stephan, F. K., and I. Zucker (1972). 'Circadian rhythms in drinking behavior and locomotor activity of rats are eliminated by hypothalamic lesions'. PNAS **69**(6): 1583–6.

Stevens, J. C., and S. S. Stevens (1963). 'Brightness fuction: effects of adaptation'. Journal of the Optical Society of America **53**(3): 375–85.

Stone, J. E., A. J. K. Phillips, S. Ftouni et al. (2019). 'Generalizability of a neural network model for circadian phase prediction in real-world conditions'. Scientific Reports **9**: 11001.

Swanson, W. H., T. Ueno, V. C. Smith, and J. Pokorny (1987). 'Temporal modulation sensitivity and pulse-detection thresholds for chromatic and luminance perturbations'. Journal of the Optical Society of America A **4**(10): 1992–2005.

Teixeira, L., A. Lowden, A. A. Luz et al. (2013). 'Exposure to bright light during evening class hours increases alertness among working college students'. Sleep Medicine **14**(1): 91–7.

Thibos, L. N., F. E. Cheney, and D. J. Walsh (1987). 'Retinal limits to the detection and resolution of gratings'. Journal of the Optical Society of America A **4**(8): 1524–9.

Tosini, G., C. Bertolucci, and A. Foà (2001). 'The circadian system of reptiles: a multioscillatory and multiphotoreceptive system'. Physiology & Behavior **72**(4): 461–71.

Tsujimura, S., K. Ukai, D. Ohama, A. Nuruki, and K. Yunokuchi (2010). 'Contribution of human melanopsin retinal ganglion cells to steady-state pupil responses'. Proceedings of the Royal Society B: Biological Sciences **277**(1693): 2485–92.

Tsujimura, S., J. S. Wolffsohn, and B. Gilmartin (2001). 'A linear chromatic mechanism drives the pupillary response'. Proceedings of the Royal Society B: Biological Sciences **268**(1482): 2203–9.

Tsujimura, S., and Y. Tokuda (2011). 'Delayed response of human melanopsin retinal ganglion cells on the pupillary light reflex'. Ophthalmic and Physiological Optics **31**(5): 469–79.

Tu, D. C., L. A. Owens, L. Anderson et al. (2006). 'Inner retinal photoreception independent of the visual retinoid cycle'. PNAS **103**(27): 10426–31.

Tu, D. C., D. Zhang, J. Demas et al. (2005). 'Physiologic diversity and development of intrinsically photosensitive retinal ganglion cells'. Neuron **48**(6): 987–99.

Underwood, H. (1973). 'Retinal and extraretinal photoreceptors mediate entrainment of the circadian locomotor rhythm in lizards'. Journal of Comparative Physiology **83**: 187–222.

Underwood, H., and G. Groos (1982). 'Vertebrate circadian rhythms: retinal and extraretinal photoreception'. Experientia **38**(9): 1013–21.

Underwriters Laboratories Inc. (2019). Design Guideline for Promoting Circadian Entrainment with Light for Day-Active People. Design guideline 24480, Edition 1. Underwriters Laboratories Inc., Northbrook, IL.

Uprety, S., P. Adhikari, B. Feigl, and A. J. Zele (2022). 'Melanopsin photoreception differentially modulates rod-mediated and cone-mediated human temporal vision'. iScience **25**(7): 104529.

Uprety, S., A. J. Zele, B. Feigl, D. Cao, and P. Adhikari (2021). 'Optimizing methods to isolate melanopsin-directed responses'. Journal of the Optical Society of America A **38**(7): 1051–64.

van Oosterhout, F., S. P. Fisher, H. C. van Diepen et al. (2012). 'Ultraviolet light provides a major input to non-image-forming light detection in mice'. Current Biology **22**(15): 1397–402.

Vandewalle, G., E. Balteau, C. Phillips et al. (2006). 'Daytime light exposure dynamically enhances brain responses'. Current Biology **16**(16): 1616–21.

Vandewalle, G., S. Gais, M. Schabus et al. (2007a). 'Wavelength-dependent modulation of brain responses to a working memory task by daytime light exposure'. Cerebral Cortex **17**: 2788–95.

Vandewalle, G., C. Schmidt, G. Albouy et al. (2007b). 'Brain responses to violet, blue, and green monochromatic light exposures in humans: prominent role of blue light and the brainstem'. PLOS ONE **2**: e1247.

Vetter, C., P. M. Pattison, K. Houser et al. (2021). 'A review of human physiological responses to light: implications for the development of integrative lighting solutions'. LEUKOS **18**(3): 387–414.

Viney, T. J., K. Balint, D. Hillier et al. (2007). 'Local retinal circuits of melanopsin-containing ganglion cells identified by transsynaptic viral tracing'. Current Biology **17**(11): 981–8.

von Helmholtz, H. (1896). Handbuch der physiologischen Optik. L. Voss, Hamburg.

Walmsley, L., L. Hanna, J. Mouland et al. (2015). 'Colour as a signal for entraining the mammalian circadian clock'. PLOS Biology **13**(4): e1002127.

Webler, F. S., M. Spitschan, R. G. Foster, M. Andersen, and S. N. Peirson (2019). 'What is the "spectral diet" of humans?' Current Opinion in Behavioral Sciences **30**: 80–6.

Webster, J. G. (1969). 'Critical duration for the pupillary light reflex'. Journal of the Optical Society of America **59**(11): 1473–8.

Welsh, D. K., J. S. Takahashi, and S. A. Kay (2010). 'Suprachiasmatic nucleus: cell autonomy and network properties'. Annual Review of Physiology **72**(1): 551–77.

Westheimer, G. (1966). 'The Maxwellian view'. Vision Research **6**(11–12): 669–82.

Woelders, T., T. Leenheers, M. C. M. Gordijn et al. (2018). 'Melanopsin- and L-cone–induced pupil constriction is inhibited by S- and M-cones in humans'. PNAS **115**(4): 792–7.

Wong, K. Y., and F.-X. Fernandez (2021). 'Circadian responses to light-flash exposure: conceptualization and new data guiding future directions'. Frontiers in Neurology **12**: 627550.

Wright, K. P., A. W. McHill, B. R. Birks et al. (2013). 'Entrainment of the human circadian clock to the natural light-dark cycle'. Current Biology **23**(16): 1554–8.

Yamakawa, M., S. Tsujimura, and K. Okajima (2019). 'A quantitative analysis of the contribution of melanopsin to brightness perception'. Scientific Reports **9**(1): 7568.

Yang, P.-L., S. Tsujimura, A. Matsumoto, W. Yamashita, and S.-L. Yeh (2018). 'Subjective time expansion with increased stimulation of intrinsically photosensitive retinal ganglion cells'. Scientific Reports **8**(1): 11693.

Yoshimura, T., and S. Ebihara (1996). 'Spectral sensitivity of photoreceptors mediating phase-shifts of circadian rhythms in retinally degenerate CBA/J (rd/rd) and normal CBA/N (+/+)mice'. Journal of Comparative Physiology A **178**(6): 797–802.

Young, R. S. L., and E. Kimura (2008). 'Pupillary correlates of light-evoked melanopsin activity in humans'. Vision Research **48**(7): 862–71.

Zaidı, F. H., J. T. Hull, S. N Peirson et al. (2007). 'Short-wavelength light sensitivity of circadian, pupillary, and visual awareness in humans lacking an outer retina'. Current Biology **17**(24): 2122–8.

Zeitzer, J. M., D.-J. Dijk, R. E. Kronauer, E. N. Brown, and C. A. Czeisler (2000). 'Sensitivity of the human circadian pacemaker to nocturnal light: melatonin phase resetting and suppression'. Journal of Physiology **526**(3): 695–702.

Zeitzer, J. M., L. Friedman, and J. A. Yesavage (2011a). 'Effectiveness of evening phototherapy for insomnia is reduced by bright daytime light exposure'. Sleep Medicine **12**(8): 805–7.

Zeitzer, J. M., S. B. S. Khalsa, J. F. Duffy et al. (2005). 'Dose-dependent response of the human circadian system to photic stimulation during the late biological night'. American Journal of Physiology **289**: R839–44.

Zeitzer, J. M., N. F. Ruby, R. A. Fisicaro, and H. C. Heller (2011b). 'Response of the human circadian system to millisecond flashes of light'. PLOS ONE **6**(7): e22078.

Zele, A. J., P. Adhikari, D. Cao, and B. Feigl (2019a). 'Melanopsin and cone photoreceptor inputs to the afferent pupil light response'. Frontiers in Neurology **10**(529): 1–7.

Zele, A. J., P. Adhikari, D. Cao, and B. Feigl (2019b). 'Melanopsin driven enhancement of cone-mediated visual processing'. Vision Research **160**: 72–81.

Zele, A. J., P. Adhikari, B. Feigl, and D. Cao (2018a). 'Cone and melanopsin contributions to human brightness estimation'. Journal of the Optical Society of America A **35**(4): B19–25.

Zele, A. J., P. Adhikari, B. Feigl, and D. Cao (2018b). 'Cone and melanopsin contributions to human brightness estimation: reply'. Journal of the Optical Society of America A **35**(10): 1783.

Zele, A. J., and D. Cao (2015). 'Vision under mesopic and scotopic illumination'. Frontiers in Psychology **5**(1594): 1–15.

Zele, A. J., A. Dey, P. Adhikari, and B. Feigl (2020a). 'Melanopsin hypersensitivity dominates interictal photophobia in migraine'. Cephalalgia **41**(2): 217–26.

Zele, A. J., A. Dey, P. Adhikari, and B. Feigl (2020b). 'Rhodopsin and melanopsin contributions to human brightness estimation'. Journal of the Optical Society of America A **37**(4): A145–53.

Zele, A. J., B. Feigl, P. Adhikari, M. L. Maynard, and D. Cao (2018c). 'Melanopsin photoreception contributes to human visual detection, temporal and colour processing'. Scientific Reports **8**: 3842.

Zele, A. J., B. Feigl, S. S. Smith, and E. L. Markwell (2011). 'The circadian response of intrinsically photosensitive retinal ganglion cells'. PLOS ONE **6**(3): e17860.

Zele, A. J., and P. D. Gamlin (2020). 'Editorial: The pupil: behavior, anatomy, physiology and clinical biomarkers'. Frontiers in Neurology **11**: 211.

Zhang, D.-Q., K. Y. Wong, P. J. Sollars et al. (2008). 'Intraretinal signaling by ganglion cell photoreceptors to dopaminergic amacrine neurons'. PNAS **105**(37): 14181–6.

Zhang, D. Q., M. A. Belenky, P. J. Sollars, G. E. Pickard, and D. G. McMahon (2012). 'Melanopsin mediates retrograde visual signaling in the retina'. PLOS ONE **7**(8): e42647.

Zhao, X., W. Pack, N. W. Khan, and K. Y. Wong (2016). 'Prolonged inner retinal photoreception depends on the visual retinoid cycle'. Journal of Neuroscience **36**(15): 4209–17.

Zhao, X., B. K. Stafford, A. L. Godin, W. M. King, and K. Y. Wong (2014). 'Photoresponse diversity among the five types of intrinsically photosensitive retinal ganglion cells'. Journal of Physiology **592**(7): 1619–36.

Zhao, X., K. Y. Wong, and D. Q. Zhang (2017). 'Mapping physiological inputs from multiple photoreceptor systems to dopaminergic amacrine cells in the mouse retina'. Scientific Reports **7**: 7920.

Zhu, H.-F., A. J. Zele, M. Suheimat, A. J. Lambert, and D. A. Atchison (2016). 'Peripheral detection and resolution with mid-/long-wavelength and short-wavelength sensitive cone systems'. Journal of Vision **16**(10): 21.

Acknowledgements

DSJ is supported by an American Association of Sleep Medicine Foundation Focused Projects Grant for Junior Investigators Award (255-FP-21), a Brain and Behavior Research Foundation NARSAD Young Investigator Grant (28056), a Knights Templar Eye Foundation Career Starter Grant, and a National Academy of Medicine Healthy Longevity Global Catalyst Award (2000012740).

AJZ is supported by an Australian Research Council Future Fellowship (ARC-FT180100458).

JMZ is supported by a grant from the U.S. Department of Defense (W81XWH-16–1-0223).

SNP is supported by the Biotechnology and Biological Sciences Research Council (BB/S015817/1) and Wellcome (106174/Z/14/Z).

Cambridge Elements ☰

Perception

James T. Enns
The University of British Columbia

Editor James T. Enns is Professor at the University of British Columbia, where he researches the interaction of perception, attention, emotion, and social factors. He has previously been Editor of the *Journal of Experimental Psychology: Human Perception and Performance* and an Associate Editor at *Psychological Science, Consciousness and Cognition, Attention Perception & Psychophysics,* and *Visual Cognition.*

Editorial Board

About the Series

The modern study of human perception includes event perception, bidirectional influences between perception and action, music, language, the integration of the senses, human action observation, and the important roles of emotion, motivation, and social factors. Each Element in the series combines authoritative literature reviews of foundational topics with forward-looking presentations of the recent developments on a given topic.

Cambridge Elements $\equiv$

Perception

Printed in the United States
by Baker & Taylor Publisher Services